Prospering Woman

A complete guide to achieving
the full, abundant life

D0169865

RUTH ROSS, Ph.D.

New World Library
San Rafael, California

Published by New World Library
P. O. Box 13257, Northgate Station
San Rafael, CA 94913

    89   11   10

Cover by Kathleen Vande Kieft

Back cover photo by Jim Konwinski

Dedicated in love to my
daughters (and teachers)
Kathy and Becky

ACKNOWLEDGEMENTS

I want to acknowledge and give thanks to the small, still voice within me that wanted to be heard and urged me to write this book. I also wish to express my deep and loving gratitude to all the women and men along my path who taught me that the meaning of life is to love. I thank my mother who gave me love along with her pans of huge, warm, cinnamon rolls that since have become legend; and my eighth grade teacher, Elsie Dwight, who taught all eight grades in one room, yet took time to inspire me to go on to college. Thank you Anne Armstrong, my cherished friend and psychic advisor. You showed me how to trust and believe in myself. Most of all, I thank Jerry, my husband, who teaches me love every day by his ceaseless patience and tenderness.

Thanks too to my family, students, friends, clients, who have shared their lives with me over the years, helping me to channel the knowledge of which I speak. A special tribute to my close friend and teacher, John Enright, a profound philosopher of life, who gave me so much. Bouquets of roses to my editors, Mary Ann Shaffer and Judy Johnson, without whose help I could not have finished the work I wanted to do. Praise to my publishers, Mark Allen and Jon Bernoff, who guided only with loving, thoughtful suggestions. To Doris Donaldson, Clara Mae Mathis, Connie Warton, and the staff who read the manuscript for technical errors, I am eternally grateful.

Thanks to Susan Vaughn, Charles and Bill Staley, Helen Bonner and Bud Camillucci who inspired and gave me strength with their encouragement. And to the many others too numerous to list here, I extend a heartfelt thanks.

Last of all, I thank you dear readers for accepting this with love,

Ruth

Table of Contents

Preface

Why A Book On Prosperity for Women?

This is a new age — the age of the Prospering Woman. Every day we are breaking more role barriers, and allowing ourselves to think independently about who we are and what success means to us. We are focusing on what we want from life, and are determined to go after it.

The purpose of *Prospering Woman* is to show you how natural it is to prosper. Prosperity is experiencing balance in life; it is attaining what we want on mental, physical, emotional, spiritual *and* financial levels. Prosperity is the natural result of opening our minds to our creative imaginations and being willing to act on our ideas. From this perspective, to prosper is a human right, having nothing to do with being either female or male.

Nevertheless, many of us have negative feelings about what it means for *women* to prosper. Why is it that the closer many women come to personal success, the more uncomfortable we become inside? Part of the answer seems to lie in how we have, until now, defined prosperity and success, and part is in the fact that as women, we are programmed and have programmed ourselves not to prosper.

Women have associated being successful in the world with being male for so long that, as we cross an invisible role line and learn to become stronger, more independent, and successful in our own right, we may feel a tightening in our gut. This feeling tells us we're getting close to the perimeters of an earlier programming. We feel the effects of our unspoken, unwritten agreement that to personally prosper is to be unfeminine.

The key to getting out of this programming is to take a new look at what true prosperity is. In the past, prosperity has been almost totally defined in traditional, aggressive, competitive male terms. It required behavior 'unbecoming' to women who have been expected to exert only their softness and have been applauded mainly for serving and supporting others.

The emerging woman finds herself in conflict with these terms or assumed values. The stereotyped male success pattern does not fit our needs. Our journey is neither to dress up like men, compete like men, or imitate men, using their definitions. We need a new perspective, a 'paradigm shift' in redefining what true prosperity and success are.

In 'new age' terms, prosperity is clearly not role or gender determined. It is the result of having developed a 'consciousness of prosperity' — realizing that as human beings we have all the tools we need to create our prosperity. It is being fulfilled in the highest sense — experiencing peace of mind as well as having an abundance of wealth, health, and happiness in life.

It is time for both women and men to be powerful and successful — not because of their sex, but because they are human. Women and men alike will appreciate and use the tools found in this book, for the principles of prosperity are the same for all. You men will not only learn new ways to create abundance for yourselves and find support for your efforts to create a success in broader, more humanistic terms, you will also understand more about the Prospering Women in your lives, and how to assist those you want to see prosper.

Women will learn how to 'deprogram' their sex role training and *allow* themselves to prosper, feeling good about it. The 'holistic approach' to abundance does not require that women deny their feminine natures. The opposite is true. *Prospering Woman* is proposing a shift in perspective — a new look at how feminine values and characteristics lend themselves to the prospering process.

For example, women have always known, intuitively, the importance of balance in designing a successful life. Many of us have watched high-achieving men reach the top financially only to find their empires crumble because their success was not balanced. This imbalance might be evident in a broken home, a wife divorcing from lack of real contact, children drifting without sincere care and guidance, friends gone from lack of depth in relationships, or health broken from too little personal attention and self-love.

Many women, viewing this picture from the sidelines, have concluded that money acquired without the balance of a satisfying, loving life is an empty gain. They have opted out, or decided to gain their 'wealth' through dependency, not independence.

This is not the time for women to retreat into dependency. This is, instead, the time for women to assert their own values and beliefs and to affirm their personal power.

World problems cry out today for all of us to help in formulating new values and perceiving new answers. The very characteristics that women have been acknowledged for, and that many men are beginning to appreciate in themselves as well — intuitive awareness, vivid imaginative processes, empathy, sensitivity, and nurturing — are all needed in order to succeed and prosper at every level of life.

These attributes are an integral part of our human nature, and an important aspect of achieving true prosperity in the world in ways heretofore undreamed of. By finally acknowledging the power of the intuitive, imaginative side of ourselves, we have access to our enlightened imagination, and to the full creative power of our minds. These are the basic tools for our prosperity.

Chapter 1

Prospering Woman

"All prosperity begins in the mind and is dependent only upon the full use of our creative imagination."

*H*ave you ever had a 'magic day' where you did something out of the ordinary and it worked? On those days, you got what you went after — no matter what it was. This book is all about how to be in touch with your creative power to make your life a succession of 'magic days'.

Prosperity is having the power to create a life of your choice — to get what you really want, not just what you're handed. We all have this prospering power and we all have experienced those special days when we knew it. Although no two 'magic days' are alike, sometimes hearing another's story can help us remember our own 'magic' stories.

When my editor, Mary Ann Shaffer, read the material in this book, for example, she understood the events of one such 'magic day' in her life. I am including her story here — the first of several 'Prosperity Profiles' — with the hope that it will serve to remind you of times when you, too, have tuned into your own prospering energy, and made 'unbelievable' things happen.

We will first need to become aware of our power of prosperity before we can deliberately bring it under our conscious control to create a life of abundance.

PROSPERITY PROFILE NO. 1

MARY ANN'S STORY

Mary Ann sat in the living room of her small suburban home in Los Angeles, feeling her usual vague sense of discontent. She wanted more of *something* in life — but she wasn't sure what it was. She watched the hands of the clock. The children were in school until three; with his new job her husband would not be home for another week. Why had she agreed to move here anyway? She knew no one in this entire city, had no special plans of her own, and there was nothing she was particularly excited about doing.

Everything seemed to close in on her that day — almost forcing a change. The weather had been bad all week — hot and muggy. The house had felt intolerably small. She wanted to get out, do something — but what? And where?

The negative thought patterns that usually led to nothing but resignation came up for her again. She considered a job, but knew she wanted to be home with the children while they were still so young. What could she do anyway? Her interests were reading and writing, her work skills limited and rusty from being home for four years. This morning, however, these thoughts weren't enough to appease her restlessness.

The 'magic' feeling started when she decided she had to do *something* — it was time. Her actions that followed from that moment made no particular sense to her, but somehow she felt she had to follow through.

In the past few weeks she had frequently allowed herself to daydream about what she really wanted. This morning it paid off. She remembered that in college she had always wanted to write. She couldn't ignore any longer that she still wanted to.

A sheet of white paper lay on the desk in front of her. She felt as if she was making a statement to the world when she declared in big, bold letters: I WANT TO WRITE. Thinking a minute longer, she added: I WANT A JOB WRITING. She remembered she didn't have a good typewriter, and thought as long as she was doing this, she might as well go all out. She wrote: I WANT A *NEW TYPEWRITER — FOR FREE.*

Suddenly, she got up and stretched. This felt better. "Why not ask for what I want — I deserve it!" What did she want to write about? Books, of course — her other love! At the bottom of the page she wrote, "I WANT TO WRITE ABOUT BOOKS — GOOD BOOKS." She folded the paper and put it in the desk drawer.

With a rush of energy, she picked up her purse and walked out the door. As she told the story later, she recalled an uncanny feeling at that moment — a feeling as if she were full of purpose.

By five o'clock that evening, Mary Ann had a job writing for *several* newspapers. Her specific writing assignment was to critique the latest books coming out in fields she was interested in. And she was the proud owner of a brand new typewriter that didn't cost her a cent. That job later developed into writing a popular column which lasted several years, and led to a whole new career working with creative writing. What had happened that day?

Although she didn't know it, Mary Ann had tuned into a *prosperity flow* — a creative energy that we all have available to us at all times. Unconsciously, she had used the laws of prosperity to bring about dynamic positive change in her life. Like most of us caught in the excitement of that flow, she didn't understand her feelings at the time.

Walking down the street she had felt puzzled. How could she feel so resolved when she had nowhere to go? She had no answer for the nagging, scolding voice inside, which demanded to know what she was doing and where she was going. Was she planning to walk up and down the street until she found a job? She ignored the voice, but she did feel foolish. Another part of her was in charge now, and she couldn't rationalize or justify it. "Why not act like a fool?" she thought. "Being reasonable hasn't always helped me."

When she impulsively entered her favorite local

bookstore, she was greeted by Sid, the owner, asking her if she had read the new Harold Robbins book. She answered, "Yes, wasn't it awful!" That remark started a conversation quite unlike any other she had had with this usually reserved man. After fifteen minutes or so of laughing and telling each other their favorite book stories, another customer, who had obviously eves-dropped, approached them. He gave Mary Ann his card, and asked if she had ever reviewed books. She said, "No," but he continued to hold out his card. He said he was the editor of several local newspapers and could use someone with her enthusiasm and insight into writing — if she was interested.

Seeing the look on Mary Ann's face, the bookstore owner, caught up in the excitement of the moment, offered Mary Ann full use of all the current books to critique if she took the job.

She thanked them both, made an appointment for the next day and jubilantly walked on air out of the store.

"Now," she told herself, "go for the typewriter." When she took her old typewriter into the appliance shop and was offered only $20.00 for it, her heart sank. The new ones were $120.00 and her budget couldn't be stretched. She had no way of knowing the other woman waiting to be helped would 'just happen' to say loudly, "If I only had a few more Green Stamps, I could get this TV set for free." Mary Ann 'just happened' to have a box full of Green Stamps in her car — two years' worth. She hated to paste them in, but didn't want to throw them away. She couldn't believe her ears when the woman offered her $80.00 for them.

The store owner, who had followed the two of them out to the car, stood fascinated. "Look lady, with this $80.00, and the $20.00 from your old typewriter — well, I was gonna mark those Olympics down to $100.00 in two months anyway. Why don't you take one of those home with you, and I'll mark down the price now."

Something special had happened that day. Mary Ann didn't have a name for it, but she knew it was special. It wasn't just the job and the typewriter — it was something beyond that. She knew she had been witness to something she had helped to create. She had done her part all right, but it was bigger than her efforts alone. She felt her whole physical being had changed — lightened. Her heart sang. Whatever it was, she knew she wanted more of it.

With the help of this book, you, too, will learn how to have more of 'it'. You will see how natural it is for us to prosper — to get what we want in life. We are naturally creative beings with far more power to bring positive change into our lives than we've ever imagined. Becoming prosperous is the result of using the full potential of our minds, the attitude we take about ourselves and our interrelations with others.

PROSPERITY AND THE MIND

All prosperity begins in the mind and is dependent only upon the full use of our creative imagination. Thought is energy, and this energy has the power of manifestation. Manifestation means to produce, to cause to happen, to bring forth from the world of ideas to the physical world of reality.

Our minds have the power to create. This power comes from our ability to imagine. Everything ever created by humans was first an imaginative idea in someone's mind. We are totally surrounded by these creative ideas manifested physically — from the cup of coffee in the morning to the TV program at night.

Prosperity, also, is a product of the creative mind. Essentially it is a state of consciousness, an attitude. Having the consciousness of prosperity is knowing that you have the ability to live a wondrous life through the full use of your creative imagination. When you are totally open to your flow of creative ideas, and are willing to act on them, you are on your path to an abundant life.

The prosperity process involves recognizing that the world we live in is only an external form of whatever we are imagining inwardly. We create the world around us as we imagine it to be. We achieve and maintain the degree of well being in the external world that we conceive ourselves having internally. The image we carry is a reflection of our belief system.

What we believe is what we achieve — nothing more, nothing less. The secret to success is to use the same imaginative process and belief system we've been using, to bring the positive changes we desire into our lives.

Prosperity cannot be forced with will power. It must be coaxed with imagination. Will power may bring momentary superficial gain, but in any contest between will and imagination, imagination always wins as the stronger force.

Once we understand the power of imagination, we understand why prosperity must exist in our consciousness before it can manifest in our lives. In practical terms, this means *before you can become prosperous, you must create an image in your mind of being prosperous.*

WHAT IS A PROSPERING WOMAN?

While no one image or concept fits every Prospering Woman, she is generally one who not only wants a full life, but also has the self-awareness to know specifically what a full life is for her. She comes to know who she is as a person, and chooses work that allows her to express herself well. She no longer needs to wait for freedom or approval, for she has found her independence lies within her own self-acceptance. Prosperity comes easily to her when she finds the secret of the ages: *her security does not exist in any bank account, but in the full use of her creative ideas.* For this reason, her focus is to learn to tap the powers of her imagination, and put her thoughts into creative action. She is then able to create the choices that come with financial prosperity.

The Prospering Woman knows that to live in a prosperous condition is to feel free to do, be, and have what she wants. The feeling of prosperity, however, does not necessarily come with any certain amount of money.

For example, a recent poll reported in the Wall Street Journal indicated that a large majority of top executives making well over $500,000 annually did not feel prosperous. For the most part, they felt insecure and worried about a multiplicity of problems. It is obvious, then, that any effective plan to achieve successful material prosperity must also include consideration of what makes us *feel* prosperous.

What makes *you* feel prosperous?

One woman I know goes without lunch to buy flowers, and feels full all day. Another prefers books to clothes. Another feels coddled when she can go out to lunch spontaneously without anything special to celebrate. It's important to know what makes you feel special, for *feeling prosperous is a way of being in the world.* It is a statement about how you see yourself and your relationship with others.

BARRIERS TO PROSPERITY

The attitudes you hold about yourself and others are the only obstacles keeping you from your prosperity.

You deserve and can have all you desire in life, but just dabbling in occasional positive thinking won't do it. *Our most powerful conceptual prospering patterns are operating at the unconscious level.*

We have become set in our minds about the scope and limits of our own prosperity, based on long-held concepts and decisions about ourselves. These thoughts, though we are no longer conscious of them, constitute a preprogrammed agenda for ourselves in our subconscious mind. We will accomplish only that which we believe deep down is possible, according to our internal picture of ourselves. For this reason, all behavioral and mental change, to be long lasting and effective, must have the force of the imaginative mind behind it.

Prosperity, then, *is an inside job — it is a matter of transforming your consciousness.* You must find ways to let go of your old negative concepts of yourself as being inadequate, unsure, victimized, unworthy — whatever stands in the way of seeing yourself as a creator of plenty.

CONCENTRATED MIND ACTION

This book is about making some unconscious processes conscious. 'Concentrated mind action' is a term I'm using to define the definite conscious use of a natural mind process that we are unconsciously using now to create our own world.

Concentrated mind action is a process applying new techniques to the old ideas of the power of the mind, to create a step-by-step procedure to unfold ways of acknowledging and releasing blocks to prosperity, and to fully utilize the powers of your mind to achieve your goals.

Humans are energy systems. We hold energy, dam it, refine it, direct it — with thought. By focusing thought, we channel the energy of the mind.

How you use this power of channeled energy will determine the quality of your life and the degree of your prosperity. Both are dependent upon the nature of your thought — positive and negative.

With concentrated mind action, you will learn to use the mind as a vehicle, a tool for your evolutionary growth. The highest purpose of the mind is to become ever more self-aware. In the process, you will learn to develop a consciousness necessary to attain and sustain prosperity as you deliberately choose to: (1) let go of negative thought patterns, (2) create a space for events of a more positive nature to take place in your life, and (3) use the power of your thoughts creatively.

PROSPERITY CONSCIOUSNESS QUIZ

Only *thought* stands in our way of attaining what we want in life. We can have what we think we deserve, and what we believe we can have. Conversely, if we are convinced we shouldn't have, or are unworthy of getting, what we want, we will also unconsciously arrange to put whatever we need in our path to prevent our becoming successful.

How do you picture your prosperity? Use the following check list as a guide for looking at your belief system about yourself. Answer as honestly as possible, and then become an unbiased observer. How do your answers indicate the ways you are promoting or preventing your prosperity?

The chapter numbers indicate where you can find information to help you develop your prosperity consciousness in each area.

Question	Chapter

There are no right or wrong answers, so never make yourself wrong for not meeting your own expectations. We are all becoming the person we want to be. If we are overly judgmental about ourselves when we receive insights, the insights stop coming.

PROSPERITY PROFILES

Throughout the book you will find a series of 'Prosperity Profiles' — personal interviews with a variety of prospering women. Most qualify their situation as being in the process of becoming Prospering Women. No one is ever 'there' or stays 'there' all the time. Nevertheless, they have that consciousness of prosperity which allows them to feel fulfilled with a sense of who they are and what they want, and they are presently living out their dreams. My hope is that you can find yourself in these pages, and can benefit from their experience.

PROSPERING RESULTS

Everyone will benefit in different ways from the ideas expressed in this book. A young client of mine named Mary was able to use the prospering concepts to overcome seemingly desperate circumstances. At twenty-nine, she was deeply depressed. Her husband had died the year before. Her sense of loss was compounded by the fear of poverty looming endlessly before her. She had two small children to support, few marketable skills, and no recent work experience. Her health was declining as a result of her depression and lack of self-care.

Using the 'concentrated mind action' process, she learned to relax, accept what had to be accepted — the finality of the death — and to work with the possibilities that life offered. As she learned to let go of the old (memories in this case), she actually created space in her life for the new to exist. She learned to take her mind off her negative image of herself, and look at who she really was. With a new consciousness, she was able to acknowledge her strengths and weaknesses, and recognize all the possibilities around her. With new-found confidence, she was able to take advantage of them, finally accepting a job which she had previously been fearful of accepting. Her health improved as her depression lifted, and she has since gone on to establish her own successful business in the same field.

As you develop a consciousness of prosperity, you will experience results from your own efforts almost immediately. We are meant to be prosperous, but like everything else, the process is as important as the end result. At first, for example, when you learn to clear your mind and focus with intent, you can experience improved mental ability with greater concentration, recall of detail, or a heightened sensory awareness.

When you are learning to 'picture' your own success, you may find yourself increasingly effective at current tasks. This will produce a more positive self-image and greater self-confidence.

Relationships improve. Learning to listen and respond to opposing inner wishes often reduces internal conflict and produces greater peace of mind. When you project a more positive inner attitude, conflict with others is reduced.

As your sensory awareness increases, you are more keenly alert to early warning signals of impending ill health. Good eating and exercise programs are more easily maintained using your mental energies in a positive way.

This book is the beginning of a new adventure. Choosing prosperity as a way of life will mean you are opening creative channels in ever-greater proportions. Financial reward is a start, but true prosperity is finding a context within which you can best express your total self. You will continually see higher and bigger challenges as you increase awareness of your uniqueness and what you truly value. By using the Keys and Laws of Prosperity, you are actually programming your mind to produce prosperous conditions in all areas of your life.

The purpose of Part I, *Releasing*, is to set the foundation for your new prosperity, allowing you to uncover concepts that are acting as barriers in your life. The 'Keys to Prosperity' will help you release the habitual thought patterns that came as part of the package of the female role: low self-image and restrictive concepts of self in relation to money, power, love, and success.

You will then be ready for Part II, *Receiving*. In a step-by-step procedure, you will learn how to use the laws of prosperity in a 'concentrated mind action' process. By combining concentrated thought and imagination, you will be able to reprogram that subconscious agenda of 'making do' for newer, conscious goals of prosperity.

Part One

Releasing

We will first look at ways of releasing negative self-images which can serve to hinder our prosperity. These negative images include concepts of self in relation to money, power, and love.

As the Zen master illustrated in attempting to pour a cup of tea for his student when the cup was already full, becoming empty is also part of the process. If you are already filled with concepts that are not conducive to prosperity, you will not be in a position to allow new ideas to affect you. We must release to prepare to receive.

Chapter 2

Prosperity and Purpose

"Money, success, power, fame, prestige, and spirituality are all interrelated — they are our inner and outer work at one and the same time."

Starting to learn about *how* to prosper without first considering "Why prosper?" would be like starting an important business trip without asking where you wanted to go, why you were going, or what you wanted to experience once you got there. Prosperity, defined as an attitude, a way of being that creates a desirable world, requires that we know what we want and why.

This is a pivotal time for women, and it is very appropriate to be asking ourselves such questions as: What do I want in life? What do I want to pursue with my time and energy that is worthwhile? Do I want to be rich and successful? Why do I want to prosper?

Giving ourselves permission to prosper, to be all that we can be, demands that we define our basic philosophy of life. When we ask, "Why prosper?" we are really reflecting on the philosophical basis of our goals.

What is the bottom line for you — why do you want to prosper? What are you trying to satisfy in your life? What motivates you to reach out and do your very best, to excel?

We all have a need to fill an existential pit of emptiness, but that is rarely satisfied with material manifestation. Many feel survival is the prime motivator, but do we need *affluence* to meet our survival needs? They are easily met with a few hours of work a week. If simple survival were the goal, carrot stew is awfully cheap.

Philosopher Alan Watts claims survival is the last of our worries. He feels the existential question in life is what to do with the nine-tenths of our time that we don't need to use in working for survival. Women are ready for something more positive than survival. We've had enough symbolic slaving over the hot stove and cold typewriter. We have a desire to feel that our lives are somehow worthwhile, that what we are doing has deeper meaning.

YOU CAN HAVE IT ALL

Life has seemed an either-or proposition to many women. Either you devote your life energies to having a career and money-making activities, or toward loving and serving others. We are learning that these goals are not opposites; we do not have to choose between them. *The spiritual, loving path leads through the world.* Money, success, power, fame, prestige, and spirituality are all interrelated — they are our inner and outer work at one and the same time.

Our human dilemma is a need to balance these two aspects of our growth — the spiritual and the pragmatic. We need to expand and reach for connection with our higher selves, to feel unity, and get a sense of direction. At the same time we need to 'ground' our insights, and express our total self in the day-to-day world in meaningful ways. If either dimension — the spiritual-emotional or the pragmatic — takes over, we experience crisis.

For example, the business person who ignores the emotional side of life often has an inner sense of grayness, meaninglessness, in spite of plenty of outside reward.

The housewife who over-identifies with her giving-nurturing side, and devotes herself exclusively to her family, is likely to sense the loss of her personal identity over time. The equilibrium is gone. She may not be aware of the inner conflict, only of being depressed and dissatisfied. She finds herself provoking arguments and being overly critical and judgmental.

The need for balance is evident again. Attaining wisdom, love, *and* prosperity need not be at odds — they can contribute to one another in a flow toward even greater personal growth. In other words, it is not only possible, it is also *desirable* to have love, wisdom, and wealth in our lives.

But why be wealthy? Is its value only in the luxuries and leisure it affords? Emerson saw prosperity in the form of wealth and power as a natural state for human beings:

> *Poverty demoralizes.... Men of sense esteem wealth to be the assimilation of nature to themselves.... Power is what they want, not candy — power to execute their design, power to give legs and feet, form and actuality to their thought; which, to a clear-sighted man, appears the end for which the universe exists....**

SEARCH FOR WHOLENESS

Webster defines prosperity as "a state of being successful with vigorous and healthy growth." If our purpose in life is unity and harmony with all that exists, then prosperity, as an inherent element of growth, is part of our search for wholeness. To prosper is to grow, to fulfill one's destiny, to be all that one can be.

Prosperity for ourselves pre-supposes prosperity for all. We are all equal; there is no one among us who deserves *more*. The laws of prosperity are similar to the light of the sun: it shines on all alike.

How can everyone prosper? That seems to contradict everything we have ever been taught. Contrary to common belief, the economic pie is expandable. We do not

---

*Brooks Atkinson, ed., *Selected Writings of Ralph Waldo Emerson* (Modern Library, N.Y., 1968) pp. 697-698.

live in a universe with limited good. Only our concepts of ourselves and of how the world is set up are limited.

We are living in a period of time in which economists say we must prepare to cut back, to do with less. They point out that our resources are used up or are running out. Unemployment rates are high and going higher, along with inflation — sure signs of recession.

While it is true that we are coming to an end of an era, it is also true that the possibilities are still unlimited in this new 'Aquarian age' we are entering. We have only begun to tap the potential of female energy, for example. This is our age to produce. We are part of the balance the world needs now.

Ours is not to lead or prosper by exploitation, but to balance the male's thrust that has catapulted humankind to dizzying heights in technology. As a result of the unbalanced development of this technology, for example, we have created the most fantastic destructive capabilities through nuclear weapons and guided missles without even thinking about the total insanity of it all.

Physical force has long been extinct as a necessary survival technique, and logic alone provides a narrow view of human affairs. The intuitive, imaginative powers of the female are needed in this strife-torn world. The thinking creative male welcomes, with a sigh of relief, the new-age woman's willingness to share in the tremendous responsibility for creating the good life.

Women have a message worth hearing. It is for us to produce, to help create a synthesis of coexistence principles by weaving tapestries of feminine qualities of love and understanding into areas of power — government, finance, and business.

Finding our own personal and universal purpose is a life goal we must discover for ourselves before we know what part of the tapestry we can best weave. Without purpose we are lost. The joy of prosperity is only possible when we know we're on our path to self-expression.

What is it that only you can say to the world? What needs to be done that can best be done by you?

In my attempt to remind myself that there is a greater purpose to life, I keep this posted where I will see it every morning:

> *Keeping in mind —*
> > *The true nature of the universe*
> > *The real reason for life*
> > *The essential core of my being*
> > *The divinity of all around me*
> *I rise each morning to meet the day —*
> *Asking to remember — all day.*

PROSPERITY PROFILE NO. 2

Collin Wilcox Paxton, actress on national television and film, Broadway and London stages, and director of the Instant Theatre Company.

Q: Do you consider yourself to be a Prospering Woman? What is prosperity to you?

A: *Yes, I do consider myself a prospering woman. Prosperity, to me, is having the ability to expand in every moment. To be able to live spontaneously in our moment-to-moment life situations. Prosperity, like my work, is never complete. When one has mastered one level, there is still more work to do; the attention to expansion never ends.*

Q: Are you aware of definite shifts in consciousness that have allowed you to expand more?

A: *Yes. I found that my ability to expand in a given moment is my ability to observe how my mind is working, and a willingness to feel.*

Q: How has this ability to expand and to observe your mind influenced your life?

A: *By the time I was 31, I had obtained many of the goals I had set for myself. I was a working actress, and had several children, and a marriage I cared about. But it was as if I was playing house with dolls — there was no depth to anything. All the old answers bored me and I didn't know any new questions. With the assassinations of Robert Kennedy and Martin Luther King, I was thrown into a deep depression and a feeling of helplessness. I had to find new meaning in life.*

I turned to Quaker teachings. It was the beginning of my understanding of 'the light within.' I began to understand what Einstein was saying: energy doesn't die. Eventually I found that in knowing myself I knew and loved 'others' and that we were one.

I discovered I was responsible for living every moment in love.

Chapter 3

The Prosperity Principle —

A New Perspective

"There is nothing either good or bad but thinking makes it so."

—Shakespeare

What if we could experience this world from a different perspective — a different point of view from the one most people have? What if this world is really set up for you, me, and everyone else to succeed — easily. Sound crazy? Yet we've all known people who have achieved prosperity in the broadest terms, whose lives seem different in that they are not struggling the way many of us are. Some of these people have discovered the *prosperity principle* — a unique attitude or point of view about life.

WHAT IS THE PROSPERITY PRINCIPLE?

The prosperity principle is a way of looking at life as if *everything happens for our benefit*. From this perspective, we learn to accept 'what is' and work with it. We stop demanding that people or circumstances change in order that we can be happy. We come to realize that the reason for any event in life is to learn something we need to know to take our next step in growth.

Interpreting whatever life brings as happening for our benefit does not mean we suddenly have no problems. It also does not mean we suddenly experience no pain or anxiety in life. We do not have a choice of whether or not to have problems in life. We will always have problems. In fact, if we ever got rid of them, we would go out and get some more. Why? Because we create them to grow by; *problems are our opportunity to grow.*

What does happen when we live by the prosperity principle is that we look for growth and opportunity in all experiences. Divorce, for example, may be a shatter-ing event but it also has the potential for positive change that possibly had been needed for a long time.

With this new perspective of looking for the lesson in 'negative' events, we are able to experience emotional pain and suffering with a different attitude. We know, for instance, that emotional pain can be an alarm indicating disharmony in the mind. Pain is often triggered by fear, caused by thought. When this is happening, the pain is our signal to release fearful thought in some area of our life.

Another outcome of living from this new perspective is learning that we cannot fail. We only choose not to go any further on a particular path. We then experience the success of choosing to let go of what is not working. From this point of view, then, our problems, barriers, chal-lenges are seen as opportunities to grow and we bless them accordingly.

THE SCARCITY PRINCIPLE

The 'scarcity principle' is the opposite of the prosper-ity principle. To those living under scarcity, there is never 'enough' in life: enough money, love, sex, power, ad infinitum. As Auntie Mame said, "Life is a banquet, and most poor fools are starving to death!" Many people feel inadequate in themselves — incomplete — and want 'something' from others but do not know exactly what. They love in order to receive. Love becomes a barter. The only thing they have plenty of is self-doubt. Success to them means someone else must lose, for there is only so much to go around. There are only winners and losers in their world.

Scarcity thinkers often feel that any significant movement of thought, idea, or behavior will result in a loss rather than a gain. For this reason, they rarely antici-pate the future with hope. They resist change by hanging onto old ideas and behavior whether they bring happiness or not. After a while, getting what they truly want doesn't even enter the picture as a possibility. They rationalize by saying, "This may be bad, but at least I know what to expect." This kind of thinking keeps us in jobs, marriages, and relationships we have outgrown and yet fear letting go of.

Many who are in scarcity consciousness resist change vigorously. We can't seem to get enough of what we don't really want once we think in scarcity.

One client of mine, Marie, had established a scarcity consciousness early in life, and was having difficulty giving it up when she came in to see me. Even though she was the wife of a very successful businessman, Marie was making herself miserable trying to live out her mother's image of the perfect, supportive, self-denying wife. Her frugality knew no end. She shopped the Good Wills and St. Vincents for bargains on winter clothes, skimped on food, and always bought the older bruised fruits and vegetables. As her husband's business expanded and there was plenty of money, Maria still could not spend — on herself or her family. She insisted on saving everything for a 'rainy day'. With increasing financial prosperity, she actually became more miserable.

The rainy day had come all right — but not in the way she had anticipated. She knew how to handle poverty — but she did not know how to handle prosperity! Life was not to be enjoyed, but to be saved for.

By acknowledging her basic fears of loss that money represented to her, she was eventually able to start enjoying her money and to use it the way it was intended — as a sharing medium. As long as she focused on how little there was in life, how far it had to go around, and how difficult it was to get one's share, Maria was stuck in scarcity thinking. Even new, prosperous events are interpreted in the poverty framework when we are in scarcity consciousness.

THE NEW VIEW

How do we view life from the 'prosperity perspective'? A Prospering Woman accepts the flow of life readily and adapts to unforeseen shifts. Being flexible, she is able to quickly take advantage of opportunities as life presents them. She sees that change is inevitable and desirable. She is open to the endless opportunities all around her. She experiences life as living in a universe filled with abundance — and gives herself total permission to help herself to her share.

She knows that her own thoughts, attitudes, and fears limit or expand her relationship to this universal abundance. She has dreams of where she wants to go based on a realistic evaluation of herself and her environment. She has a live-and-let-live attitude toward others: cooperating, assisting when she can, and releasing when she can't. She knows she has a choice, and she deliberately chooses to focus on what is possible instead of what isn't.

Most of us slide into and out of both the consciousness of prosperity and scarcity. We are always in the process of expressing one or the other. To change scarcity thinking we need to recognize the signs of it: fear, anxiety, and worry. By releasing these emotions, we have a choice of seeing all the benefits in each situation, and gathering valuable information for the next step in our growth.

PROSPERITY PROFILE NO. 3

Pauline Cotten, 33 years old, is owner of three profitable gift shops called the Calico Cat, in the San Francisco Bay area.

Q: What do you think is the key to your success in business?

A: *I never let things get me down. I take things as a lesson. Ever since high school, I've had this thought in my head, "If three bad things happen, something good will happen." And sure enough, it would! You have to believe there is something good coming down the road for you.*

Q: How did you start thinking about going into business for yourself?

A: *After college, I tried working for someone, but found out right away I didn't like it. I took stock of my talents and skills. I knew very little about retailing. My father had been in business for himself and I admired what he did. Some people think what I've done is special. I don't think so. I just did a lot of thinking about it. I got very specific about what I wanted. I decided exactly what kind of store I wanted. I developed it around a specialty item that no one else had. I was the only one in the area with this concept of selling. I resisted all outside pressure to include other items and it has paid off. Now the customers come to me specially for what I have. I enjoy being different.*

Q: Were you afraid of taking the risks involved in starting a business?

A: *I learned in incremental steps. I started small so I made mistakes and learned on a small scale which I could apply as I grew.*

Chapter 4

Successfully Winning

"When we experience true prosperity, we experience acceptance by the world as worthy. This is difficult for us before we have accepted our own worthiness."

Abe Lincoln once remarked that, "People are about as happy as they decide to be." Women, too, are about as prosperous as they decide to be. Developing a life of abundance is the result of deliberate decisions. Women have traditionally blocked their prosperity consciousness with decisions which led to self-defeating attitudes about self, money, power, and love.

By following the suggestions in the next four chapters, you will be able to review your decisions in these areas, which may uncover and so help you to change those attitudes presently blocking your prosperity. The concept of ourself is our first concern, for that is the basis of all other attitudes we hold.

FEMALE AND SUCCESSFUL?

The first concept to decide upon is whether it is ok for you, as a woman, to prosper.

We have identified and celebrated masculinity with the idea of 'success' for so long that many women have forgotten the obvious: prosperity is not gender-determined by nature. Being prosperous has nothing to do with being either female or male — it is a learned cultural role.

Once we start to challenge the limitations set by the cultural assumption that being female and successful are mutually exclusive, we are on new territory. It is no wonder, then, that one of our first concerns in becoming a Prospering Woman is how the men in our lives will respond to our success. We have a wide range of fears connected with this issue of invading their 'domain'. Some of the more effective fears we use to block our path to prosperity are such ideas as:

1. To be successful we must become masculine in attire, attitude, and behavior.
2. If we climb too high, too fast, in the business world, it will be assumed that we granted sexual favors en route.
3. As single women, our success will threaten men and we won't attract life partners.
4. Marriage relationships will be endangered if we start to earn more money or have more prestige than our mates.

The reaction of males to our new roles *is* mixed. Many men totally applaud and support our more expansive roles — others don't. Because of their own fear, many men do feel threatened by the so-called new 'macho-woman'.

It is not the attitude of men with which we need to be primarily concerned, however. Any real change in life always starts from within. It is our own attitude that demands our focus. We fear the reaction of others only when we believe, at some level, that what they are saying is partially true. The key to prosperity is to change *our* minds — our thoughts — about ourselves and our success.

Most women do not want success to be a barrier between themselves and men. Whether it is or not will depend primarily upon our inner decisions. The challenge is not on how the men will react to us but on overcoming our own fear of failure, fear of success, and lack of self-worth. When we feel good about our own prosperity, so will the rest of the world.

OVERCOMING FEAR OF FAILURE

When I believe my value as a human being is gauged by the results of my actions, my self-esteem is vulnerable. My fear of failing at any act is intensified.

Fear of failure is the fear of being or doing some 'wrong'. It presupposes there is a 'right'. Yet, how can we fail when there is no way of knowing, on the grand scale, the ultimate outcome of any single act we make? How many things in your life which you thought were total disasters turned out to be the best thing that could possibly have happened?

Fear of failure keeps us from risking, but a willingness to risk is a measure of our prosperity consciousness. When we're blocked from this consciousness by low self-esteem, we are unwilling to try something new. Rather than be open to opportunities, we suffer from doubt and mistrust of our abilities and tie ourselves in psychological knots when faced with even the thought of stepping out, moving ahead, and taking a chance with the unknown, the unproven.

In doubt, we identify more with the possibilities of failing than of winning. We seem to be saying, "If I don't reach too high, I won't fall too far." In our unconscious minds, we're imagining failure far stronger than we can see, smell, or taste success.

One way out of this fear is to ask yourself, "What is the worst thing that could happen if I failed at something I really wanted? What would be the ultimate calamity?" Ask yourself if you could live with the worst possible result.

The trick is in specifying the fear. Usually the worst never happens. It rarely happens to the degree that our active imagination conjures up. By specifying the fear, however, the rational mind has something concrete to work with in helping dispel the fear. As long as the fear remains nebulous, it continues to have power over us.

Every successful person agrees that the risk is the fun of achieving. Our highs in life come not from having or doing any single thing, but from the strength we experience when we find the means within us to face a challenge and overcome all barriers to resolution. Prove this to yourself by thinking back to a time in your life when you were the most elated. What challenge did you have to overcome to achieve that success? We get energy from taking a risk once we face our fear, and act in spite of it. We forget that when we risk, we might lose, but we *sometimes win!*

Yet winning can establish a fear of its own — the fear of success can be just as paralyzing as the fear of failure.

LOOKING BENEATH THE FEAR OF SUCCESS

Have you ever felt like stopping just when things got going good? Did you feel confused about this conflict?

We all have impulses urging us to open up, move on, communicate more, give more, be more. At the same time, we can have an almost equal urge of restraint — a feeling of wanting to pull back. Why? This is often the fear of success.

Fear of success has sometimes been called the fear of the sublime — the fear of acknowledging that we really are great and wonderful beings. That idea is more than many of us can stand. *Being prosperous comes too close to proving it is true.*

Think how your lifestyle would change today if you truly believed that you were a great and glorious person with something valuable to contribute. How would you live? How would you act with your boss? How would you dress? What colors would you wear more? What basically would be different about you? Everything we do, say, and have expresses our beliefs. An image of success could require radical change to our basic self-image that we're not ready to handle.

If success should come before the self-image is ready for it, we will do whatever is necessary to put the brakes on and discredit it. When we experience true prosperity, we experience acceptance by the world as worthy. This is difficult for us before we have accepted our own worthiness.

Success also brings with it great expectations by others. It is easy to assume it is our responsibility to fulfill these expectations. Ironically this can fuel the fear of success — we may yet fail!

Fear of success is a barrier to the development of our prosperity consciousness when it keeps us from developing our full potential. To the degree that we fear personal success, we tend to also separate ourselves from the successful. Those who dare to risk and achieve remind us painfully of what we're not doing. To avoid this pain, we condemn with envy and jealousy, or we admire with awe. Both responses separate us from others.

Only when we are able to truly appreciate *and enjoy* the success of others are we setting up the right mental attitude to be successful ourselves. Each time we sincerely applaud others for their achievements, we can rest assured our own success is coming closer *because our consciousness is on success.*

Your way out of fear of success is to realize *you are in control.* It's just as it is in skiing: once you know you can come to a stop, you can let go! All true success is personally defined. You decide the goal, the pace, and the parameters around which you are willing to be successful. You call the shots. You have only you to please in your success.

YOU ARE WORTHY

Fear of failure and success stems basically from lack of self-acceptance. Every successful woman must go through the crucial hour of facing herself squarely and declaring her own independence to herself. At that point in time, she must accept all her foibles and weaknesses, along with her beauty, strength, courage, and know-how. This is her moment of true liberation. It is a statement of the end of waiting in line for approval. We all know the power of self-approval. Until we reach the moment when we are able to give ourselves complete approval, however, we block our prosperity consciousness with our self-doubts and feelings of not being good enough.

Women have no edge on the market when it comes to feeling low self-esteem or feeling unworthy. It seems to come with being human. Women, however, have been considered second class, and very few of us have escaped that gnawing feeling that we've never quite made it. This is a perfect set-up for scarcity consciousness.

The prettiest are never pretty enough. Our bodies are either too big or too little in the places that count. If we don't know math, we're not smart. If we do know math, so what? It seems as though we can't win. Some of us have tried to compensate for a low self-image by being the best at everything — super-woman at home, in relationships, in school, or on the job. Too often, this only covers up those deeper feelings that somehow we have to prove ourselves to someone.

Sound familiar? It all comes from scarcity consciousness, from not feeling 'good enough'. For whom? For ourselves, of course.

Psychoanalysis focuses on the original causes of how we started all this, but if we are to get any immediate real change in behavior, we need to focus more on how we are daily reinforcing this negative state of mind — and on the effect of finally letting it go. While in this state, we substitute wishing for doing. This wishing is often in the form of repetitive thoughts about ways we are inadequate. How many people do you know who think that if they dwell on their faults and fears long enough:

1. This is somehow almost as good as improving;
2. Maybe some magic will happen and they will overcome their bad habits automatically;
3. No one will criticize them because they are saying it first; or
4. Someone will at least take pity on them.

What they don't realize is that by dwelling on miseries — internally and externally — they are unconsciously inviting even more negativity into their lives. The process by which this works is, paradoxically, the same process which provides the way out of low self-esteem:

Prosperity Key No. 1

We Reap What We Sow

Our lives manifest our dominant thoughts. Just as whatever we plant grows, that which we focus our attention on multiplies. Whatever we put into our minds comes out in our lives.

By deciding to only focus on, and move toward, what you want, you are able to raise your self-image. Each time you dwell on inadequacies, you decrease your self-assurance.

When we plant the idea in our minds that there is not enough in life, we reap scarcity. When our focus is on loss, past pain, and fear, we get more loss, pain, and suffering in return. To understand how this works, let's go a little deeper.

WE'RE ALWAYS WINNING

As Richard Bach wrote, "Argue for your limitations,

and they are yours." Some people have a life theme of believing that they can't have what they want in life — and they often don't get it. This gives the impression they are losing in life, when in fact they are winning.

This kind of winning, however, acts as a block to prosperity consciousness for it is negative winning. How does it work, and how do we remove this block? The answer is in this key:

Prosperity Key No. 2

We Always Prove Ourselves Right

We all have the need to be *right*. We want to *prove* that whatever we believe is in fact *true*. That's the nature of consciousness. If we have an unconscious low self-esteem, we will need to prove ourselves right and produce a life that supports that internal image.

It is uncanny how we mastermind a life plot that 'proves' we are 'no good'. Depending on what the script calls for, we can: get caught, hurt ourselves, get pregnant, get fired, lose something important, over-spend, get drunk — whatever is appropriate to prove we're 'no good'. When we've really *proved* it, we've created a win! A negative win, but a win. We showed the world we were right all along.

We select circumstances that occur in our lives by choosing how and where we focus our attention. For example, when we concentrate on reasons life doesn't work and why we can't have what we want (my husband won't like it, I don't have any money, I haven't the time, I'm too old anyway, I just can't, etc.), we remain oblivious of opportunities to change our circumstances, and so perpetuate our negative 'wins' — i.e., your husband *doesn't* like it, you *don't* have any money, there *isn't* any time, and you *are* too old.

WINNING POSITIVELY

The law of causation is the same for both positive and negative wins. They are both produced by thought; only the emphasis is different. A positive win is created when we realize that within every problem lies the solution. It is our choice how we interpret every event. There is no one way to look at any set of circumstances.

Almost everyone has a favorite story of someone who has turned adversity into opportunity. Those who benefit from the calamities in their lives, whether it is an accident, a divorce, or a loss of some sort, are people who prefer positive wins. They create positive results from even the negative circumstances of life by choosing to focus on what they *want*, and on what they *can* do.

As long as we are content to substitute negative wins (proving we can't) for positive wins (proving we can) we effectively block our prosperity consciousness. Before we will move out of low self-esteem and give up negative wins, however, we will need to recognize the 'pay-offs' or benefits we receive in them.

The single biggest pay-off for negative wins is getting to play 'martyr', and we will go to great lengths to play that game. For example, when we stay with an alcoholic mate who has no intention of changing, we may be expressing a need to be 'put down', or to feel like the 'healthy one' in a relationship, or to perform the miracle of changing another. We may have an axe to grind, such as choosing men who reject us, and thus prove that all men are brutes, or we need to prove that we're unlovable.

If we assume that all life is growth-oriented, we would have to agree that we are always moving toward the expansive, the positive. We choose whatever we think is best every moment, according to our state of conscious awareness. *The basic underlying reason for every act then is good — only the means create the negative results.* The more conscious we become about who we are in relation to all life, the more directly we can get what we want in a positive manner.

If we are all moving toward the positive, then why don't we believe what our own eyes and ears tell us about the negative situations we're in? Because, unconsciously, until we get the 'message' of the negative situation, we will do whatever is necessary to remain in the learning situation!

We repeat our negative wins until we're clear about what we want, or at least don't want. Then we are ready — with energy built from the experience — to go on to our next step. *We change internally so we can tolerate a different life externally.*

The sooner you can find your pay-off in any negative situation, the sooner you can speed up this learning process. Once you become aware of the name of the game you're playing, the easier it is to let it go. This frees you to get on with positive wins.

Use this prosperity key of always proving yourself right to identify any negative self-image you may be 'proving'. Look at every negative situation as if you were winning — *somehow* — even if it is difficult to see how this could be. *Do not blame yourself.* Ask yourself, "How is this a win for me? What am I getting out of this that I couldn't get faster any other way?"

As soon as you give yourself permission to prosper, step through your fears of failure and success, see that you deserve all that you desire, and move toward what you want, rather than toward what you don't want, you are deciding to win successfully!

PROSPERITY PROFILE NO. 4

Mara Marin, divorced with one young son, has created a unique employment referral business, WHIM. Four years ago she started with $12,000 capital and a good idea. Today her business is worth over $100,000.

Q: As a successful woman, how do you relate to men?

A: *It's been a problem all my life. I was smart, intelligent, quick. For a long time I thought I envied men. Now I know it's not men I envied — what I envied was that if you were a man, you could use your brain to get ahead. As a woman,* not *using my brain was supposed to be an asset.*

As a teenager, I tried to figure out how not to be smart or competitive. Eventually, I had to maintain my integrity and be who I was — not play a role. There was a lot of pain around coming to terms with that question.

Q: How did you resolve that in your own mind?

A: *The answer for me was in recognizing that first I am a person. I'm not a woman first. Now I say what I feel and don't stop to check in to see if it's a female point of view.*

There was pain not only in relationships with men, but also with other women. I have found it difficult to relate to women who have chosen to remain passive and uncomfortable with their own assertiveness, especially when they appear to be threatened by my self-expression.

Q: How do you handle men who are hostile to successful women?

A: *Basically, I'm a non-threatening, perceptive person. I don't think others feel the need to feel competitive with me. I approach all people as equals.*

I also watch my environment. Emotional prosperity to me is recognizing my needs. If I'm uncomfortable with people, I choose to avoid them when I have a choice. It's great to experience choice in life. Men and women have both created the sexist wall we have. There's no percentage in blaming each other.

Q: Did you ever feel you had to give up your feminine qualities to be a Prospering Woman?

A: *Definitely not. I appreciate my deeper feelings. I frequently express my compassion in business, for example. It's not meant just for home and children. It's meant for the world. I believe that being in business and being human are not separate. If I speak to anyone from an open, sensitive, articulate place, they will most likely respond in kind. Prospering to me is acknowledging we all carry responsibility for our financial and emotional well-being.*

I also use my intuition frequently in making decisions. I know that each decision I make is the best solution I can perceive given the factors of time, commitment, money, and my feelings.

Q: Have you ever felt the need to dress in a more masculine way in order to prosper?

A: *In the long run everything is superficial, you know — what you wear, what kind of car you drive. We women need to look at ourselves regarding the games we play with dress and everything else. I had to ask myself if I was wearing a filmy dress or blouse to relate to the male in the old role or because I enjoyed wearing it. Now I know that I dress to please myself.*

I am not appealing to the man's protection when I go see my banker, for instance. I state the purpose of my visit, what I want, what I have to offer. I ask if we have a place from which to negotiate. I don't patronize him and I don't want him to patronize me. Sure I'm a woman, but I don't apologize if I don't know something. I haven't had the experience a man might have had. I just state what I want, and ask what's the next step.

We then negotiate, not because of my dress, but because we will both benefit.

Q: What was your biggest barrier to becoming a Prosperous Woman?

A: *Understanding that I deserved the rewards of my labor. Sooner or later we have to recognize that being humble just doesn't work. I was taught to give; it's difficult to receive.*

Chapter 5

Money Is the Means

"Everything reflects our consciousness, and there is little value in staying in the consciousness of poverty."

*P*rosperity has had only one connotation for too long — money. In previous chapters we have redefined prosperity in more holistic terms; now let's take a new look at what money really is.

The subject of money has a powerful emotional charge, equivalent to the subject of sex. Yet, we will usually talk about it only like the weather — in general economic terms. In this age of open discussion on homosexuality, menstruation, and incest, it is interesting that we are still very closed in what we reveal about our money. The subject of our inner feelings concerning money is one of the last things to come out of the closet. Why?

When we think of having money, we think of opportunities for independence, leisure, privacy, time to do and act as we wish. Unfortunately, a lack of money translates into yet another reason to put ourselves down.

We have built a complex of myths and voodoo around the idea of money as an entity — an end in itself. We have personified it, and attributed characteristics to it as if it were a savior. How many times have we said, "If only I had enough money!" At the same time, we have created a concept of money as an active, negative agent. We have done this through our conscious and unconscious myths which support a negative morality system about what money does to people. We end up both desiring and fearing money.

I can remember a time when I didn't want to talk

about money, or even think about it. I felt squeamish asking for money due me. And in establishing a price for anything, I always hoped that somehow the other person just 'knew' how much was fair so we would not have to discuss it. I even fancied what it would be like to live in a community of total barter, so no money would have to be exchanged.

It wasn't until later that I found out I wasn't alone — many people are uneasy when they must receive, ask for, and speak of money. Fortunately, there are different ways of looking at money: what it is, and isn't; what it can and can't do. Examining our concepts of money can open up issues concerning giving and taking that are important in all aspects of life.

The basis for understanding and being comfortable with money is just one more aspect of our self-awareness. For example, from repeated studies in human behavior, we know that one of the factors by which we judge ourselves and others is money — how much we make, how we make it, and how we spend it. This constitutes part of our 'market value'. To many of us then, speaking of income is really speaking of our 'value'.

When we have a low self-image, we sometimes try to compensate for these feelings both by trying to increase our 'value' and by trying to keep this 'value' hidden. We want to avoid facing a low opinion from others if our value figure is not as high as we think it *should* be.

An example of wanting to hide our 'value' is deciding not to invite people to dinner because we have only mismatched glasses and china. When we are devaluing ourselves from lack of money, we may feel ashamed at gatherings of friends or family who talk about travel, shopping, or prestigious colleges for the kids. We may put ourselves down because we don't have the money to shop or travel, or because our kids are only going to work, instead of college.

THE MORALITY OF MONEY

The self-esteem and money issue is further confused by the rather shaky image of what having that 'green stuff' means. Although everyone wants more money, the idea of having wealth is tainted. On one side of the coin, money is thought to be highly desirable; on the other side, it is considered bad and almost 'dirty'.

Most of the cultural arguments making prosperity a moral issue are never made out loud. The ideas that we can't or shouldn't be financially prosperous are projected subliminally in the form of myths or beliefs. Whether we live it or not, one of our strong Judaic-Christian beliefs is that hard work and toil are rewards in themselves. It is also part of our tradition that poverty is a virtue. Religious teachings from the Bible have even been interpreted as confirming that poverty is somehow 'holy'.

For example, "Blessed are the poor in spirit, for theirs is the kingdom of heaven," has been frequently quoted to condemn wealth and praise poverty. With better understanding of the old Arabic translations, however, new interpretation among biblical scholars shows that the original intention of this and other passages was positive. With new research, we now know the word poor originally meant *humble* and *receptive,* not poverty-stricken. To receive is to open oneself to one's vulnerability — to let go of control. The message seems to have been that the world is full of givers; what we need to learn is to receive — to open ourselves to our vulnerability.

Other passages, such as, "It is easier for a camel to go through the eye of a needle than for a rich man to enter the kingdom of heaven," have been used to prove that being wealthy is morally wrong. According to modern-day scholars, this passage originally referred not to having money itself but rather to the difficulties inherent when we are controlled by our possessions rather than being in control of them.

Everything reflects our consciousness, and there is little value in staying in the consciousness of poverty. Someone has remarked that the best thing we can do for the poor is not to be one of them. This is not being unloving. It is a statement of not accepting poverty as inevitable. Poverty helps no one.

Other biblical passages point out another, more prosperous attitude toward life:

> *"Ask and it shall be given you;*
> *Seek and ye shall find;*
> *Knock, and the door shall be opened unto you."*

Environmental support for the negative attitudes we hold about wealth is found in clichés we often hear repeated:

> *"Money is the root of all evil."*
> *"Money won't buy you happiness."*
> *"Easy come, easy go."*
> *"I may be poor, but I'm happy."*

I'm sure you can recite many more. They imply that not only is there something wrong with money, but, by implication, there may be a lot more wrong with *you* if you have it!

WHAT IS MONEY REALLY?

Money is commonly defined as a medium of exchange. What we are exchanging is *energy*. Money is a concept symbolizing the exchange of potential energy. It is stored energy made visible.

It is obvious that, like everything else, money is in itself neither good nor bad. It is neither moral nor immoral. To look at money as a moral issue is as absurd as it is to decide that airplanes are good or bad. We feel differently about airplanes when they are used to drop napalm bombs than when they are used to drop food supplies for starving people. Yet they are the same planes. The moral issue is in the *intention* of the user — not in the plane itself. Money can be used to promote life, and love, and can be a blessing for many, or it can be used to destroy the life force in a million different ways.

MONEY AS WHORE

Accumulation of wealth has long meant having more than one's share, and gaining at the expense of others. We are reminded of the 'Robber Barons' of all ages — companies and individuals whose assets are the result of exploitation. The 'get-rich-quick'ers with a 'to hell with the means' attitude have poisoned our minds about money with the beliefs that (1) what one has to do to gain wealth is to steal, and (2) wealth (i.e., greed) ruins the human soul. When we point to those who misuse money selfishly as proof that money is bad, we are confusing the pirate with his ship.

A ship is indifferent as to who is at its wheel. It responds just as swiftly to a scoundrel as to a saint if both are equally skilled in the laws of sailing. Carefully loaded, its hull will carry contraband arms to thieves just as safely as it would emergency medical supplies to a disaster area. Ships, like money, are just there to be used as resources. How some people in the past have used them does not change their value.

When we are prospering naturally, we are using a holistic approach to achievement within a 'win-win' position. We do not need to rely on taking from or exploiting others. *With this kind of prosperity, loving money is loving the good it can do for us, and for everyone else.* Prosperity in this sense is appreciating money as a means for exchanging good for all.

MONEY AS POWER

Money brings power. Money has no power in itself, but having control over how it will be spent gives us power. The more money we have, the more potential power we have.

Goethe said, "Nobody should be rich but those who understand it." His point is that many can become prosperous quickly, but not always develop awareness, scruples, or concern for others. They can lose their money just as quickly, or in some way pay dearly for it, if they do not develop their prosperity consciousness.

If we are going to ask for power in great amounts, we had better be prepared to handle it. An example of what happens when we are unprepared for the power of money emerged during a recent follow-up study of the million-dollar lottery sweepstake winners in Canada. The vast majority of them were broke within five years. Their prosperity consciousness was not developed to the point where they could benefit from the money for very long.

You will either control or be controlled by money. Awareness of the power of money, and of how to handle it, makes the difference. It is the conscious choice to use money benevolently that puts you in control.

MONEY AS RESPONSIBILITY

The stored energy that money symbolizes is there to help us grow. This energy must keep moving. Effectively directing this movement of energy requires an understanding of how the laws of prosperity operate in giving, receiving, spending, and saving. Responsibility of money is knowing where we want to go with this energy.

Prosperity Key No. 3

To Receive More, We Must
Be Willing to Give More

Money doesn't grow by being hoarded. Hoarding is for beggars. It doesn't benefit anyone to grab as much as possible and keep it stashed away in vaults or coffee cans. Trying to prosper by bottling up money through accumulation will result in the opposite negative effect. We hear tragic stories of those individuals who die each year in poverty with their 'wealth' stuffed in their mattresses. It served no one, least of all them.

In all of life, receiving depends upon giving. There are no separate rules for money. All spending is part of the circulating flow of giving — *when done in the right spirit*. Try it out. Next time you spend, see yourself as giving to benefit others as well as yourself. Spending with love can be a new experience. Just as work can be love in action so, too, money can be love expressed. When we give in this spirit, our return is multiplied many times.

Spending is no problem for some people. It can be too easy, in fact. After a few experiences of succumbing to the temptation of unlimited credit, leading eventually to unlimited debt, they quickly discover the pain of over-spending, of being out of balance at the other end of the spectrum.

Part of the responsibility that goes along with the power of money is knowing how to save and invest for a purpose. Ralph Waldo Emerson, for example, saw money as a 'stewardship', or challenge. To him, each person with money has a mandate to use that money to 'carve out' work for others.

How do you use money? What plans or direction do you see for your money? What seeds are being planted with your money?

If the farmer has no plan, and throws her seeds hither and yon, she not only wastes her resources, she has only a small crop in return. And she cannot tend her crop if it is scattered. Start planning for your future now by investing in yourself. Spend some time today thinking about how you *feel* about money. Ask yourself:

> *Are you willing to create the money your life dream would cost?*
> *What is 'being poor' to you? How does that feel?*
> *How do you feel about wealthy people?*
> *How do you feel about earning 'a lot' of money?*
> *How do you want to receive your money?*
> *How do you want to help others with your money?*
> *How are you uncomfortable around money?*
> *What do you want to have achieved with your money when you die?*

Far too many people never sit down and think concretely about these kinds of questions; yet, for prosperity, it is vital to know your feelings about money. How do you *feel* when you spend money? Pay attention the next time when you pull out your billfold or checkbook — are you spending from a sense of loss or giving? Listen to what you are saying to yourself as you hand out money.

What is your attitude about giving? When is it easiest to give? When is it hardest to give? Listen to the clichés ringing in your ears during your transactions with money. Our attitudes toward money are often indicative of our attitudes toward life itself. Do you give freely of yourself? Is it hard for you to receive?

In order to achieve prosperity on a continuous basis, we must develop *balance*. Momentary desires will have to be balanced with long term goals; savings, spending, and investing plans will have to be devised. Prosperity requires *planning*, *clear intent*, and *commitment*. Becoming friends with money and recognizing what it can and cannot do for us is an important preliminary step.

Money in itself cannot make us happy, but with intention it can provide the means of unlimited good for ourselves and others.

PROSPERITY PROFILE NO. 5

Jana Janus, graphic artist, owner and operator of Janatype, a typesetting and graphic art service.

Q: Do you feel like a Prospering Woman?

A: *Yes, for the first time in my life I can say I feel prosperous. It's all due to a career change I've recently made. Before, I had been trying to scrimp, save, sell everything I had, piece by piece to afford to do what I love to do — organizing and leading rafting expeditions. I finally figured out that I could do what I wanted without giving up everything, or working longer hours. I needed to receive more for the hours I did work. Once I became receptive to the idea of a new type of career, I soon got a chance to learn an entirely new skill. This skill brought me more money than before with less hours.*

Q: You are referring to typesetting?

A: *Yes, but it's more than typesetting. The entire scope of graphic arts is now available to me. Typesetting brings me into contact with people who are doing books and all manner of interesting projects. This means that I can use all of my art training and sense of design. I even have the opportunity to learn camera work. I'm doing everything right up to handing the work over to a printer. I wouldn't have believed last year that I would be doing this — but it's exactly what I was looking for.*

Q: You went in the back door toward what you wanted.

A: *Yes. In my being, I'm an artist. I had wanted to incorporate art with a meaningful type of occupation. I never wanted to sit in a tower and paint. I wanted art plus something. It's not surprising I arrived at this. I've done a lot of putting pictures and words together. As a kid I made picture books and sewed them together with yarn. I made little books for my children on their lives.*

Q: What decisions are you aware of that led you to your prosperity?

A: *One decision I made two years ago still sticks in my mind very clearly. I saw a Dover catalog at a friend's house. It had many wonderful drawings, wood-cuts, and lithographs — all copyright free material. I poured over it with delight. I remember saying out loud, "I want to be doing this kind of thing." From that moment, even though I didn't know the meaning of the word, I started to see myself as a 'graphic artist'.*

    I called up the local college and examined their course outlines for 'graphic art'. I was determined to know more about this work. The real changes in my life started to take place, however, when I decided to deal with issues around money. I started thinking about what money meant for me. I enrolled in an EST seminar called "About Money," where I heard that money is a way of expressing oneself. But I went beyond that. I started to put attention on my whole attitude toward money: how I paid my bills and spent my money. I began to realize that I was standing in my own way of prosperity by my feelings and thoughts about money. I had been holding a negative attitude toward money itself.

Q: How did this prevent your prosperity?

A: *For years I was a righteous hippy — anti-capitalist, anti-everything. I had never accepted much of anything. If it was 'this', I was 'that'. Those experiences were deeply important to me at the time; but I began to realize I had a whole dynamic inside me that was anti-anything that was going to elevate me. I could not see myself successful.*

During this time of 'inner work' on money, I began to develop an internal trust that no matter what happened, I would have 'enough'. It was the first time I put money in the realm of spirit. I was finally able to see what I was doing through a series of drawings I did. I drew pictures to answer the questions: "How do you see your money trip right now?" and "How would you like it to be?" The first picture came out as a large gray funnel with paper money dropping in the top, but only coins falling out the bottom. I realized that was exactly how I felt about money in my life. No matter how much came in, it was always an inadequate amount by the time it went through my system.

The second picture, on how I wanted it to be, was done with every pastel color of the rainbow. It had a big 'source' — a circle of light and love — in the center. Spiralling off this circle, or 'source,' were colorful appendages — each a different shade of the rainbow. Each appendage had the word God, hearts, or dollar signs on it.

This is how I wanted to see money in my life. I wanted it totally connected to me in a spiritual, loving way. Until then, my picture of money had been that it was a harmful weapon. It was a tool that people hurt each other with. I wanted to see it in abundance — lots of it, with loving intention on it.

I had never experienced abundance in any way in my life. I had thought that money came from one source — my job. I had thought that all my money must squeak through that little job tunnel. From my drawing, I saw that money can come from any number of sources. I can still feel how that idea scared and shocked me. Abundance is vast — infinite.

What's happening now is that I am doing typesetting for all my friends, old and new. Every single job has been filled with love and caring; I am affectionately dealt with. Last week I got a card from a friend I had done work for, saying "You're wonderful." That's the kind of energy I'm dealing with in typesetting — and earning lots of money besides!

I drew that picture depicting what I wanted, and that is what is now happening!

Q: You created the picture, and now the picture is creating your experience?

A: *That's right. And talk about abundance! Nearly every person I meet wants some kind of typesetting done — Money is coming at me from all sides — in the form and manner I wouldn't have dreamed possible a few years ago.*

Chapter 6

Power, Responsibility, and Prosperity

"Whatever you can do, or dream you can, begin it. Boldness has genius, power, and magic in it."

—Goethe

*P*rospering women are powerful women; they have made friends with their personal power. They did not *become* strong; they acknowledged the strength they already had.

Personal power is not aggressive, muscular, manipulative or authoritative power, but an inner power that comes from knowing we have all the resources we need to handle whatever happens in life. When we have personal power we shift from the pseudo-strength of appearing strong to the real strength of feeling strong. An example of this for me is being confronted with criticism from powerful men I admire, and being able to remain objective. It is a personal victory every time I do not cringe in self-blame, or feel the need to lash back at 'unjust' criticism in a defensive manner. When I'm coming from a sense of my own personal power, I can listen, be open to the truth that is coming through, and release the rest.

With this inner strength to face our challenges, life is accepted on its own terms. With personal power we engage in the dance without having to be the choreographer. Coming from strength, whatever happens is ok because we're ok.

Women have always had the potential for all the personal power they needed. They have always been strong; they had to be. By withstanding the centuries of being told they were the weaker, ineffectual, dependent, non-assertive half of the human population, they proved their strength. Even in the face of these charges, women have always known, deep down, they were capable, strong, smart, assertive, rational, and decisive.

The only change in the power of women is that now we are beginning to acknowledge this strength and take it, en masse, into the 'male world'. We are making that leap from experiencing 'inner strength' to accepting responsibility for our lives.

With that leap in consciousness we are rejecting the 'trickle down' economic theory we all grew up with. Under that theory we believed that men had power by nature, and that women would benefit most by pleasing the men in their lives. In this way, a woman was encouraged to seek power through osmosis — to be content with the power achieved through association with a strong male.

The reason this theory has lasted so long is that we saw our gains, and ignored our losses. It felt good to think there was someone wiser and stronger who could always answer our questions and take away our pain.

Obviously, there are several major flaws in this system. For one thing, in order to make it work, women have to actively throw their power away. We hand out fistfuls of energy to anyone we allow to have control over us. Psychologist John Enright uses an analogy of the trained falcon to illustrate living under the illusion of powerlessness when operating from dependency. The falcon, after making a strike, always returns its prey to the master and then gratefully accepts its small strip of flesh from the kill as reward. Dependency has been trained into the bird until freedom is forgotten, and the source of food is associated only with the master. When we become dependent, we forget that we are our own source.

We also give away power to those we feel are superior to us. The world is only a reflection of who we are. In order to see admirable characteristics in others, we must already have them in ourselves to some degree. We are potentially all that we admire; there is no need for females or males to deny personal power and separate themselves as superior or inferior beings.

The second major flaw in the 'trickle down' power-through-association theory of female-male relationships is that women lose their decision-making power when they deny responsibility for themselves, for the two go hand in hand.

One difficulty during this period of transition when women and men are finding new paths together is that many women want to keep benefits from both roles. They want the freedom to make decisions and still be protected and provided for. The answer seems to lie in women developing an even greater sense of personal power within themselves.

PERSONAL POWER — HOW TO GET IT

Prosperity is experiencing more choice in life. But choice only has meaning when we have the power to handle the consequences of our choices. The question therefore is: *How can we increase our power to have more choice in our lives?*

Personal power is dependent upon having a strong sense of integrity. The root meaning of integrity is to act as one. When we act from integrity, our desires and actions are aligned. The power that comes from acting with integrity can be likened to the power of a group pulling a rope in one direction, versus split action by the same group pulling in different directions. We have much more 'pull' when the desires of our body, mind, and feelings are integrated.

Personal power comes from within and depends upon you approving of you. Your approval comes from your sense of integrity — a total honesty within yourself. It is being who you are without pretense — acting on what you truly feel. When you live with integrity, your actions, words, and intentions are congruent with your values. You believe what you are saying and doing.

Lack of integrity creates a sieve out of your pot of personal power.

THE POWER OF INTENTION

Being honest about *intentions* with oneself and others is a basic ingredient of personal power. Keeping agreements is an example of being honest with oneself. For instance, there is always a good 'excuse' for being late to work or to an appointment. Even when the other person accepts your excuse, however, you feel an internal 'scrunch'. You know the truth that you *could* have made it had your intention been clear. If the appointment had been the last possible time to receive a free $10,000 bonus, you would have made it on time! Pay attention to how you feel the next time you give an excuse. No matter how good you are at acting justified, you devalue yourself inside when you don't keep your word, and your sense of integrity drops. Our energy contracts rather than expands when our integrity drops, so less integrity means less power.

Personal power is increased by becoming clearer in our intentions. As we get hungry for more power, we quickly learn the importance of saying yes only to those agreements we intend to keep. This plugs some of the holes of that sieve fast.

Taking responsibility is another way to increase personal power. This next prosperity key tells us how:

Prosperity Key No. 4

Our Personal Power Formula Is:
$$E = M C^2$$
*(Energy comes from seeing My
Contribution in every situation)*

If we live as though the world is against us, we don't experience much power. If we want increased power, we must assume responsibility for what we do, and don't do, in every situation.

Taking responsibility has been considered a male attitude — and one that often seemed more a burden than a blessing. Many women did not recognize the hidden 'goodie' behind responsibility was being in charge as the decision maker. The interrelationship of power, responsibility, and prosperity can be simply stated as 'The Buck Stops Here!"

When I take *responsibility* for the circumstances of my life, I am acknowledging that I created those circumstances. The more responsibility I accept for the consequences of my actions, the more *power* I am assuming. I did it, so if I don't like the results, I can re-do it.

The more power I accept over all circumstances of my life — as consequences of my actions — the more prosperous situations I can *choose to create*.

Responsibility is a position — an attitude toward events. You either take responsibility, or you feel victimized by the world. Your choice of whether to play the victim or to take responsibility will determine whose power grows — yours or someone else's. If you take the position of victim, you lose power. If you choose responsibility, you have power then to do something about what's happening — to choose your next step. *It is all in attitude.*

For example, if you take responsibility for your husband's leaving you (when you didn't want him to), you are psychologically free to look at the ways you helped set up the relationship so he would want to leave. You then learn quickly what you don't want to do next time, and you benefit from the experience.

In the past we have blocked our prosperity consciousness by rejecting responsibility because we confused it with blame. When we're stuck in 'victim consciousness' we often refuse to assume responsibility because we think: (1) If I'm responsible, then I am to blame, or (2) If I take responsibility, then the other person gets off scot-free.

Blame has no place in prosperity thinking. Blame is only a judgment — superimposed on the event. Blame is anger at oneself for feeling stuck. Blame leads only to further blame. Look at areas in your life where you may still be holding anger and blame. You will need to decide if you are willing to let go of these negative feelings for your own benefit.

For example, parents have always been the recipients of our blame. Few of us want to acknowledge we had much to do with our own up-bringing. Parents are the reasons why we aren't the sweetest, nicest, most generous, lovable creatures imaginable. If our parents had only been half-way what we 'needed' them to be, we would probably have been a president by now — or at least not nearly as neurotic. We often feel ruined for life by what our parents did or did not do in raising us.

As long as we sing this old, sad song — true or untrue — we are cutting ourselves off *today* from our power far more effectively than Mom or Dad could ever have done.

The question of whether parents are to blame is not important. It is time to get on with life, and the way to do it is to assume responsibility. Coming from a position of responsibility is to say, "I got my parents to treat me the way they did — given who they were."

We always bring out certain traits over other traits in people. For this reason, no two children are usually treated alike in the same family. Without blaming yourself or your parents, you gain in power every time you can identify the choices you made in attitude and behavior and the benefits you received by creating your formative life.

The truth is we started projecting our desires and personality into our circumstances at a very early age. If you don't believe a kid has power, try feeding a six-month-old infant some cereal when she isn't hungry. You get it all back — double! Parents did what they did, and we did what we did. It was a two-way dance.

One way out of this negative, blaming cycle is to pretend, just *pretend*, you chose your parents. If this crazy idea were true, what benefits would you have received from your choice? What lessons did you learn *fast*? In what way are you a better person from having learned these lessons? This is the type of responsible thinking that allows you to release a negative, blaming attitude.

We have the choice of experiencing the temporary power that comes with acting from anger and blame, or we can recognize the pain of a particular situation, look at what we did to help create the situation, and put our energy instead into positive planning for moving toward what we want now.

As we begin to take responsibility for ourselves, to follow the $E = MC^2$ Key, we are more open to signs and signals from our environment giving us better directions. Our senses are activated as we open up to our intuition. With more complete information and increased personal power we automatically make better decisions. Because of this, we are now ready to start creating a world that fits us better.

PROSPERITY PROFILE NO. 6

Shakti Gawain, author of *Creative Visualization*, seminar leader, author, publisher.

Q: Do you see yourself as a Prospering Woman?

A: *Yes. To me prospering is aligning myself with energy flow and universal life principles. It is feeling the flow of energy of money, appreciation, enjoyment, and the excitement of challenge. I love the process of manifesting my creative ideas into form.*

I used to feel constricted, as if there was never enough money, time, or anything. I would hang on, tightly. Now I experience total trust in the universe and know it is supporting me as long as I keep tuning into my intuition and acting on it. Prosperity is to me a sense of trusting the higher self within me — letting go of fear. This means I can risk, try new things, spend money, venture into new areas, and change my lifestyle without feeling insecure.

The actual amount of money I have is relatively inconsequential to me when I have this inner security. It is more important that I am doing what I love, and then the money seems to follow. I now spend very little time doing what I don't want. Another thing that is important to me is creating free space and time in my life — time to just be quiet and tune in. Before I got in touch with the prosperity principles, I was always too busy doing what I thought was important rather than trusting what I really felt like doing, moment by moment. Now, when I get uptight, I stop and ask myself what I need, what I want, what I feel. I may find I want to take a walk, get a massage, be with a friend — and I'll do it.

When I nourish my own self I find miracles happen. I notice the next day that I have lots of energy to take care of my outside needs because I've taken care of my inside needs.

Another way that I feel prosperous is in the feeling I have that I've contributed something valuable to other people. That gives me a deep sense of satisfaction, of fulfillment. Until I wrote my book I often felt, "Someday I want to do something significant." Now I feel I have done something. There is still plenty to come, but writing a book caused a definite shift in my life. Because I feel I've made a difference, I've fulfilled some sense of purpose in life; I experience a satisfaction that can't be taken away.

Q: Can you identify the changes in consciousness that caused you to create a prospering life?

A: *I think it came in two parts. The first part was when I became willing to take total responsibility for my life — to give up being a victim of life. Prospering thinking was realizing that no one does a thing to me that I don't in some way attract; no one has power over me unless I give it to them. If there are things in my life I don't like, I can change them. I am the co-creator (with the higher power) of my life. Believe me, taking responsibility didn't happen overnight. It was a slow process of 'trying out' the principles of responsibility. But when I did, everything shifted radically. Each step is important. Each step is learning. Each time I 'tried' I became more conscious, and could more clearly see the principles of how life works.*

The second part was my conscious commitment to growth. I made the decision to follow the truth inside me, to give up anything to follow and act on it. I saw that by making that commitment, a higher force would teach me everything I needed to know. The act of that commitment is the single biggest major cause for my prosperity. There's no turning back. I can no longer blame any outside force for my not following my own inner guidance. The pay-off has been better relationships, further openings in my spiritual life, money, success of all kinds. Everything is improving. Love and appreciation are there. I feel healtheir and more beautiful than ever. I am happy, and excited to see what unfolds next.

Chapter 7

Love, Dependency, and Prosperity

"Your love belongs to you; you take it with you; you only share it."

Being prosperous is feeling fulfilled — 'filled-full' with a sense of life and love. In this state we are no longer searching for love, we are living love.

Ironically, to enjoy this emotional abundance, we must release our intense 'need' for love — a major block to prosperity consciousness. As long as we stay in 'scarcity thinking' we will never feel loved enough. When we feel 'needy', or deprived, our desire for love seems to outrun our supply.

Before discussing ways to avoid or release the repetitive cycle of scarcity thinking about love and relationships, let's look at how cultural training contributed to starting these cycles.

ACCEPTING THE ROLE

How have we allowed our need for love to supersede our other needs, drives, and desires required to pursue prosperity?

It started very early, when we were petted, curled, told how sweet we were, and given dolls to play with. We got the message, and most of us liked it. We were girls; that meant our destiny was tied up with getting a Daddy to go with our play-house.

We were groomed, and groomed ourselves, to catch a 'love'. Taking on characteristics of self-responsibility, independent thinking, and self-confidence was left to our brothers. Women are here to find someone to please.

Men are here to provide, to be responsible, and to make us feel good about ourselves.

We bought this game. That's an important point to remember — that we did buy it, in different degrees and in different ways. There were benefits in accepting that receptive, pleasing role; we were to be provided for, taken care of. A bargain was made.

What we did, of course, was to set up total dependence on the 'great provider'. Everything depended on the reaction of the male toward us. Our whole sense of rightness, of goodness as a person, of being of value to the world, depended upon a man's 'love'.

LOVE AND NEED

It is really hard to love someone you need. Without developing a strong inner-core feeling of independent strength, a centered awareness of self — separate from our partner — our 'love' is more likely to be conditional. Most of us confuse love and need. Love is a spontaneous, pure outpouring of feeling, coming from within. Although we attribute others as being the 'cause', love comes when we have developed our capacity to feel love within.

Your love belongs to you; you take it with you; you only share it. Love is self-generated — an extension of your inner being. There is no 'bargain', no 'exchange' in love. We love for love itself.

What we have called 'love' in a relationship is very often a fulfilling of needs — a feeling of being grateful that we are being provided for, both in physical survival needs and in emotional-psychological needs.

We limit our growth and potential experience when we confuse love with protecting and providing. Love then becomes the fulfillment of a role we have established. When we come together out of *need*, it can be to feed each other's weaknesses. For example, if you choose a partner because he can plug a hole that exists in your personality — e.g., you're shy of meeting people so you (perhaps unconsciously) marry an assertive out-going partner who plays that role for you — then you never have to grow in that area.

Even in this new age when both women and men are taking time out to find who they are as people — separate from their roles — we still resist giving up the great myth. There must be some 'Shining Knight' or 'Giant Mama' who is going to save us from ourselves — to help us avoid learning what we need to learn in life, to validate us painlessly so we won't need to grow.

UNCONDITIONAL LOVE

What we are all looking for, of course, is that elusive unconditional, uncritical, and non-judgmental love. What we all need to understand is simply: it starts within. When you let go of the judge and jury within, you will find a perennial garden of love.

Prosperity Key No. 5

We Are All We Need Because
We Are What We Desire.

You are already it. *You are love;* that is your true nature. Letting go of the great search for the perfect love, and looking within instead for your own reservoir of love can free up tremendous amounts of energy which are then available for redirection.

As we begin to see the truth in this key, we also see that the female's compulsive desire for a providing, protective 'love' is a deterrent to prosperity consciousness. Until we women come to understand to what extent we have been programmed to feel like women only when we are taken care of — when someone other than ourselves loves and accepts us — we will not even be free to desire true prosperity. That very concept will instead be threatening to our basic life structure built around the idea that women are first and foremost in the serving, giving role.

LOVE AS SERVICE

To many women, work has been a filler — a 'holding place' while we waited for life to begin. Many intelligent, creative, well-educated women have devoted years of their lives in voluntary or part-time, entry-level, low-paying jobs in order to carry out the image of themselves as servers.

In many cases, the jobs themselves were taken so we could do a double shift of serving *and* providing in our promotion of the well-being of others. These jobs were attractive because they had the benefits of non-commitment and high mobility, and they were often short-term. All of this allows women to increase their support services but does little to promote the future career of the woman.

It is amazing how many young college women of today are still not taking themselves seriously. They do not see themselves having a career, but rather see themselves "in English," or "in History" temporarily, until they get married. Although the trend is lessening, the college programs drawing the most women students are still teaching, nursing, and secretarial. This still continues, in spite of the fact that the job market in teaching is at its lowest ebb, few secretaries make it up through the ranks into better paying positions, and nurses as a rule feel underpaid for the tremendous amount of work and responsibility they have. None of these factors is deterring enrollment in these three areas.

As prospering women, we must recognize that even with twenty years out for raising a family, the average woman will work twenty to thirty years of her life. Realistically, for most of us, our life income and lifestyle are directly related to our job choice. Marriage no longer precludes working; half of all married women are working, often in low-paying clerical jobs. Even after ten years or more on such jobs, many of these women still picture themselves as 'temporarily employed'. Now, with half of our marriages ending in divorce, we see the added necessity of planning a work career with sufficient financial reward to support the family we are often left with.

For you to be prosperous, you will have to deliberately choose to be. You will have to re-evaluate your life priorities, and take yourself, interests, and career seriously. You will have to look at your traditional role as server and giver to others, and decide what you want to give to yourself. In other words, you must re-evaluate your 'love priorities'.

Prosperity Key No. 6

Love Yourself First

We have been taught from early childhood to "Love thy neighbor as thyself," and we have been given some idea of what "love they neighbor" entails. But somehow the "love thyself" part has been sadly neglected — or worse, it has been given negative, narcissistic connotations. Many of my women clients have had difficulty even comprehending how to start to love themselves. I recommend a copy of this list to be put up on the bathroom mirror, to be reviewed each day, for a healthy reminder of the person we must love first:

I Love Myself

I listen to what I want and I respond to that want

I make my own rules to live by

I give myself credit often

I surround myself with beauty

I create an abundance of friends

I nourish myself with only good food

I allow myself to have abundance in all ways

I reward myself appropriately

I trust myself

I give myself pleasure in a variety of ways

I enjoy the sensations of my body

I enjoy my sexuality

I forgive myself

I give myself authority

I have fun

I talk to myself gently

I regard my needs, wants, goals, and welfare as being as important as anyone else's. *

The beautiful lesson to be learned about love is that loving yourself does not take away from loving others. It is a prerequisite before genuine love can happen. Love only multiplies. I can only give that which I have. Unless I create love within, I have little to share with others.

---

*I recommend *I Deserve Love* by Sondra Ray (Celestial Arts, Millbrae, CA) for more information about these ideas.

LOVE, SEX, AND DEPENDENCY

A discussion of women and love and how they relate to prosperity is not complete without looking at the role sex plays as a driving, motivating, satisfying force for women. An interesting theory among some sex therapists is that women must have plenty of what is sometimes called 'P.S.A.' — pleasure, security, and approval — before they feel really fulfilled.

Trouble starts when we attempt to satisfy all three needs with our sexual relationships. Trying to meet security and approval needs through sex detracts from the pleasure sex naturally brings, and can make a stew out of our self-image. It sets up the possibility that we will feel insecure and disapproved of when we don't have a good, frequent sex life with a partner. When that happens, making love can become a desperate need for improving our self-esteem. Sex has then lost its value as a unique and separate experience. The experience of *wanting* to make love, versus desperately needing to make love to satisfy a suffering ego, are extreme opposites.

Prosperity is providing security and approval from within. Feeling we have to wait for someone else to give us pleasure is yet another way we experience dependency.

As one sex counselor, Grace Darling, points out in her seminars on human sexuality, the female is complete in herself sexually. The female body is built for pleasure and she need never feel deprived. The clitoris is the only human organ whose sole function is giving pleasure. Women, therefore, do not *need* a man to experience sexual fulfillment. When we learn to separate the need for sexual satisfaction from the need for approval and security, we are free to be completely with a man in a loving, giving way — not because we need him, but because we want him.

It is only when we learn that we can give ourselves pleasure, security, and approval that we then come from a centered place and can be *totally* with a man without trying to figure out if he loves us 'enough'. We experience true prosperity when we have already done that for ourselves!

PROSPERITY PROFILE NO. 7

Joy Van Pelt has been married to a pilot for 20 years, and has four children. She works for a company that sells travel packages to large companies as sales incentives. Her job as trouble-shooter with these groups takes her around the world with top business executives.

Q: Your job sounds exciting and challenging. Have you always been independent and out-going?

A: *As a young woman, I was very independent. Something happened after my marriage, however. I reverted into a child-like, irresponsible state, waiting in my little suburban house for my husband to come home so I could start to live each day. There was always a part inside, my survival instinct, that kept saying, "I don't like this," but I would use liquor to stifle that voice. I gave my husband the father role. As a mother, I became an active over-achiever. Eventually my buried feelings became so painful I became an alcoholic to try to suppress them.*

One day, stone sober, I got a glimpse of my choice point. I 'saw' a clear image of a playground slide, and I knew I could slide down — way down — or I could turn around and walk back down the steps. I chose the steps.

Since that moment, it's not been easy to find out who I am. I had to allow all those 'cries' in my heart their say. As I changed my role in the family and with friends, all the roles around me changed, sometimes with great anguish for all of us. But there was no turning back. I no longer wanted to be a nursemaid; I saw that I couldn't be responsible for anyone else's happiness. I stopped rushing in to make everything right for everyone. I saw that I had always come last in my own life — everyone else came first. And I also saw that I was acting from guilt — living a life of how I was 'supposed to be'.

Q: What was the hardest part of your change?

A: *I knew I couldn't let go of my old behavior patterns until I found my pay-offs. I soon saw that there was a lot of power involved in my old role. If you're responsible for everyone else's good, you are powerful. That was hard to give up. Now, however, I'm feeling good about being responsible for myself. When people ask me, "How can you leave your kids?" — which I do for a week or so at a time for my job — I tell them that they are much more mature because of it. My husband does more things with them now too. I kept the older ones as children far too long. I only saw my option as being a wife and mother or nothing, and worried about what would be left for me once they were grown up.*

One good thing about learning to prosper so late in life is that it is so exciting. I almost have a 'born again' feeling. Sometimes when I'm out running in the morning, I feel the wind in my face, and the strength of my body, and I say to myself, "I'm so grateful to have lived long enough to experience this new aliveness!"

Chapter 8

Prosperity and the Mind

"There is nothing in the moving world but mind itself"
old Hindu Sutra

*H*ave you ever stopped to notice the over-flowing abundance of nature and wondered if you too were born to prosper naturally? We have all we need at birth to develop into the miraculous mental and physical beings that we become as adults. Doesn't it make sense that, like the rest of nature, we would be equipped at birth with all the seeds necessary for our prosperous growth?

If prosperity *is* a natural condition, why does it seem so hard? Because, unlike the rest of nature, we humans must exercise choice in the development of our prosperity. Unlike plants and other creatures in the animal kingdom, we are self-aware, with the ability to choose to develop a higher consciousness. Choice then becomes the means and the end because *our* growth — our prosperity — comes from our choice in the way we use our minds.

We are part of nature, but we are not blown by the wind and planted in the earth. We can decide where and when to plant our seeds. They are under our control. We can live a life being a victim, being dependent, responding automatically, or playing it safe in every way, and we will survive. But if we want to plant those seeds of prosperity that we were all born with, we must deliberately choose to do so.

The source, or seed, of all prosperity is in the full use of our creative mind. By mind I mean more than brain. Our brain is only one small part of our mind. The mind refers to the information received from the *total self* — the mental, physical, emotional, and spiritual self. The extent to which we choose to listen to and act upon the information from this mind is the extent to which we will prosper.

Your thought, in the form of intuitive hunches, dreams, and gut reactions, is your connection with your total creative mind. To help you act on the information given by your creative urges, you can begin by understanding the power of thought.

Here are four major points to consider when starting to use the power of creative thinking:

1. *To develop your consciousness of prosperity, observe every day how you are creating with your thought.*

We first create in mental form everything we desire to produce in physical form. Look around you. Everything you see at this moment that is human-made — whatever you wear, sit on, eat with, live in — was once only an idea in someone's mind. Think back over the last thing you created — a cake, a manuscript, a clean house, a painting, peace between two people — everything you do has the same beginning. It starts with a thought in your mind. It may happen so fast you don't notice it, but every move you make is preceded by a thought. We can literally say that *we are our thoughts.*

Review your day today. The quality of your day reflects the state of your mind. On days you feel up and high, everything looks terrific, even if it didn't yesterday. When you are feeling good, you produce good work.

The power and pervasiveness of our thought is so incredible that it is awesome to try to describe. There is nothing that has been invented, discovered, or achieved that did not start as an idea. Every war, public program, or miraculous physical feat had its origin in thought. Thus we are totally surrounded and affected daily by the results of concentrated consciousness from hundreds of thousands of people whose minds came into agreement to produce our cultural accomplishments — bridges, buildings, systems of all sorts. These projects are further proof of the power of collective thought.

Just having the original idea, of course, is not enough to manifest it into material reality. Ninety percent of our ideas die upon conception, or soon afterward. At best, ten percent survive long enough to become somewhat developed, and perhaps five percent see the light of day.

CONVINCE YOURSELF AND YOU CONVINCE THE WORLD

Even developed thought alone is not enough. It must be combined with belief. Unless you believe in your idea, it will die. Thought is the striking of the match, and belief is the keg of dynamite — the power behind the creative thought. Intention is the hand that strikes the match. You must know what you truly want — what your intention is — or you end up setting off kegs of dynamite in all directions as if they were firecrackers on the Fourth of July. Everybody enjoys firecrackers — but their effect is short-lived. *Getting what you want out of life requires aligning thoughts, beliefs, and intentions.* Your actions will then automatically bring your desires.

What does this mean to us?

It means that no matter what our history, we are never helpless victims. We have the power to change, to be what we want to be, to have what we want to have. That power is our thought. When our thoughts are repeated often enough, they form a pattern. These thought-patterns actually program our minds. Whatever we are programming our minds to create, they create.

2. *For a thought to be generative, it must be sharply outlined or defined in the mind.*

We tend to think about our wants in vague, undif-ferentiated, dream-like states, without putting much mind-energy behind them. That is because we find it difficult to believe that we can have what we want in life.

Wishful thinking has little power to manifest, but that isn't its purpose. A wish is only a spark — it is similar to the starter on an engine. You couldn't drive your car around the block using your starter, but that's not what it's meant for. If you really wanted to read a book, would you try to do so with a match when you have a candle?

The real power of manifestation is in the conscious and unconscious state of *expectation*. What we *wish for*, and what we *expect*, must be deliberately combined in order to create in reality positive prospering conditions.

Belief systems are the basis of our expectations. Changing our expectations to align them more with what we want now may require challenging our beliefs. We don't give up our beliefs easily, however.

The painful part about growing is always this constant challenge to our belief systems — our concepts about what makes life work. The pain comes from not wanting to let go of a position that has helped us get to wherever we are. Beliefs are a two-edged sword. They motivate us, keep us highly charged and moving, and at the same time, limit our access to other horizons.

Examples of limiting concepts I heard as a child — "Life isn't a bed of roses, you know!" and "What you want and what you get are two different things" — indicated to me that I should expect pain and misery in life, and not much of what I wanted.

Actually our whole concept of reality is limited until we experience the fact that *the only reality there is, is what we tell ourselves.* What we believe, we become.

Because we act as if our beliefs are true, they have both positive and negative effects. When we perceive the world as a finished product with the rules and decisions already made, we walk around on egg shells, trying to 'fit into' this world, fearful of disturbing the pre-existent order. Wouldn't it be more fun to sense this world as a giant pile of raw lumber just there for us to help create something better? This attitude would bring out the creative power we were born with. We want to allow our dreams to become clearer, and learn to expect to win, to really make a difference.

YOUR SUBCONSCIOUS POWER

3. *In order to understand your creative, manifesting power, you need to differentiate between the roles of the conscious and the subconscious aspects of the mind.*

The conscious mind has the task of deciding what we want to create in our lives. It does this by sorting out our thoughts, judging and discriminating among them. Using past and present knowledge, plus all the input of the senses, it weighs evidence, makes priorities, and plans for the future. Best of all, it is under our direct control.

Not so the subconscious. Our knowledge of this aspect of mind is limited: we both fear and stand in awe of it. The subconscious was long ago acknowledged by Carl Jung and others as the power base of our being, the real source behind our creativity.

We are wary of being controlled by this power, especially when we feel pulled into actions that we do not consciously accept as beneficial. At those times it seems as if our deep-gut desires have taken over completely, ignoring our rational decisions. When that happens we feel controlled by the subconscious, yet almost helpless to stop it.

Harnessing the incredible power of this machine, the subconscious, is what manifestation is all about. The task is one of the most exciting and rewarding challenges of our lives. Even at this moment our actions are being determined by this nucleus of energy — how wonderful if we could be in the driver's seat handling the reins!

HOW YOU CREATE

Our subconscious mind is basically composed of 'pictures' of all our conscious thought-patterns developed over a lifetime. Any pattern of thought that is allowed to remain in our conscious mind long enough will eventually 'sink into' our subconscious as a symbol representing those thoughts. All worries, fears, strongly felt desires, convictions, or beliefs that feel like they are a 'part of us' are the kind of thoughts we usually keep around long enough to slip into our subconscious. When they do, they form a belief system stored in symbolic imagery. These images, which we have programmed in over the years, run our lives by unconsciously determining our actions and bring to us the positive or negative conditions they represent.

The subconscious mind is subjective in nature. This means that, unlike the conscious mind, it does not discriminate between thoughts. All are treated equally. The essence of the conscious thoughts that have penetrated the subconscious are therefore accepted subjectively, without concern for their being right, wrong, good, or bad. If the conscious mind has said so, it is so to the subconscious.

The conscious mind soon loses access to these old thoughts, concepts, and decisions; but the subconscious never forgets. Change comes only when some new thought with a stronger emotional impact 'seeps through' from the conscious mind to counteract the first directive. In the meantime, the subconscious is moving the organism, robot-like, toward the programmed goal.

In this way, the subconscious is similar to an automatic pilot device that has been given coded messages about how to run a ship over the years, and is responding accordingly. All is well until the needs of the ship's captain change, and she finds the automatic device has rusted in place and no one knows how to reprogram it.

The importance of realizing the subjective nature of the subconscious is to understand that the subconscious cannot say NO. It is our impersonal 'genie' who can only reply YES, totally accepting conscious thought as an absolute dictator. *Whatever the conscious mind dwells upon becomes the orders for the subconscious to produce.*

That is both good news and bad news. The bad news is that because our culture, as most others, is so negative-prone, most of our programming has been influenced by negative thought — not only our own thought but all of those around us. From birth, we have experienced daily a bombardment of negativity from parents, teachers, peers, fellow workers, and mates. Their intention is not negative; they are the result of their own negative programming too.

Nevertheless, the results are the same. It is all too easy for us to discuss in great detail what is wrong with us and others — what we can't do, what they did wrong, what we should have done, ways we ought to change, and why we can't. By clinging to our negative thoughts, we have unwittingly allowed these attitudes to slip into the subconscious and dominate our creative energy.

Proof that our thoughts affect us, in both positive and negative ways, is easy to find. Faces, bodies, and actions of people around us reflect if they are happy, self-achieving, fulfilled people. When you are thinking joy, you are emanating joy all around you. Conversely, if your mind is absorbed with worry, doubt, and fear, that shows too. We attract or repel people according to our thoughts. When you think negatively, you turn away joy and love.

The good news is that we now have a chance to modify all this negativity in our lives. We can do it through deliberate, continuous, conscious cancelling of negative thought and substituting positive patterns.

4. *The thought most deeply impressed upon the subconscious creates what we manifest in our lives.*

It is our choice, and within our power, to deliberately select the thoughts we consciously hold.

By consciously repeating strongly desired thought-goals for a sufficient amount of time, we are actually programming our subconscious to produce that goal. Once programmed, this great impersonal computer has no choice but to produce, without question, what we ask for, indefinitely.

This is where the role of the will plays its crucial part in manifesting. Many have mistakenly tried to use their will to push, shove, and force behavior to conform to their decisions of the ideal. *The true role of the will is to be a guardian over our thoughts.* Its task is to make sure that all our thoughts positively support our goals. By keeping negative thoughts out of the conscious mind, the will is being used on the highest level possible.

Sound like positive thinking? Yes, it is, but it is more. The head, heart, and gut work together. It is not enough to mouth the words about 'good' in our lives, nor just to think the thought. We must seek it actively, feel it, and live it.

This is far from a 'Pollyanna' approach to life. The negative cannot and should not be ignored. It is to be learned from. We need to not only acknowledge the negatives in our lives, but take responsibility for them, and see what we're getting out of them.

Resisting or hiding from pain may provide momentary relief, but it assures a lifetime of pain. Facing our problems may bring momentary pain, but brings a lifetime of relief. Working through negatives and living a negative life are two very separate things.

THE POWER OF CONSCIOUS THOUGHT

Because prosperity depends upon the full use of our creative imagination, we need to find ways to fully use the *conscious* mind. Our task, as of this moment, is to become aware of our own negative thoughts and deliberately cancel them with our will power. Cleaning up our act from the inside means just that — staying with our own process and watching what we are telling ourselves.

To do this, we need to be constantly alert to the power of our thoughts, to know that there is no such thing as a casual statement. Every time we make a statement we are reinforcing our future. Words are energy and energy is creative. As Emerson said, "Words are alive; cut them and they bleed." We will use this aliveness of our own words to create life and spirit for achieving our life goals. In order to creatively use the conscious mind to reprogram the subconscious, we will need to find ways to keep the conscious mind clear. We need to be able to have: (1) concentration with clarity, (2) peace of mind with quiet serenity, and (3) the ability to be present — *now*.

We block the full use of our conscious mind when we try to experience life through 'filtered' consciousness, 'drifting' consciousness, or the 'chattering mind'. Let's look at each in more detail.

FILTERED CONSCIOUSNESS

We often misunderstand the nature of the conscious mind, and try to succeed by being a totally rational person. We strive to know 'enough' to win in life. The conscious mind, however, is a gatherer. After it has done that, its job is basically over.

The general public values information gathered by the conscious mind. Facts, figures, and hard data seem far more real to many than intuitive guesses, prophetic dreams, or gut reactions. In spite of this, top leaders in every field easily recognize that many final decisions must often be made on information that goes beyond the facts. After the figures are gathered and digested, big decisions are usually made with intuitive leaps of the imagination. We ultimately decide by what 'feels' right.

To stay more in touch with our intuitive feelings — the source of prospering decisions — we need to go beyond interpreting our experiences through the 'filter' of the conscious mind, by constantly using it to classify, computerize, and decode information from our environment. We need to 'feel' our experiences — *be* with the trees and the flowers, instead of just naming them — trusting our gut reactions to people and problems.

DRIFTING CONSCIOUSNESS

Reprogramming the subconscious requires a disciplined mind. To fully use the conscious mind for this purpose, we will want to awaken to the effect of 'drifting' consciousness.

Drifting consciousness is a way we have of disappearing mentally. When we are not 'present' mentally, we are not available to all that is going on and we are not fully prepared to change if it becomes immediately necessary. Being here — now — is hard work, and absolutely necessary for prosperity consciousness. We must be present to act spontaneously, ready to take our next step when it shows itself.

So much of our time is spent in drifting consciousness, and in distraction, without even being aware of it.

Each time we are driving down the road and suddenly 'come to', not really certain where we are or where we've been, we can be sure we have been functioning on automatic. We usually did not *choose* to reminisce, but instead were chasing an elusive thought that took us farther and farther away from being alive to the moment. Each time this happens we will want to gently re-focus the mind on the ever present now.

CHATTERING MIND

The third consciousness trap that prevents clarity of consciouness is the 'chattering mind'. In its usual undisciplined state, the mind has been likened to a 'drunken monkey', jumping about at random, going from one subject to another endlessly, producing little more than fatigue or, at best, escape. This is the opposite of the kind of directed attention necessary for prosperity consciousness. Prosperity demands concentrated thought. This idea is summed up in:

Prosperity Key No. 7

Quieting the Mind Promotes Directed Action

The incessant repetitive thoughts that obsess our minds are a drain on our creative energy. Are you aware of constantly talking to yourself? Take the next two minutes and write down all the thoughts that are going through your head. Note how unimportant most of them are, and how you repeat yourself.

You probably won't be able to write fast enough. Sit in front of a clock and try not to think for 60 seconds. Don't be discouraged by the results; you would have the powers of a very sophisticated yogi if you could stop your mind for just three minutes. Fortunately, you don't need to be a yogi to reap the benefits of quieting your mind.

A simple and effective way to stop the chatterer in your head is to say STOP! to yourself when you hear your reverberating circuits going around endlessly. An even more effective, and longer lasting, technique is to meditate. If you are a beginner, take 15 minutes each morning, close your eyes, breathe deeply, relax your body, and when thoughts come, just announce to yourself, lovingly, "Peace, be still." Meditation is a form of acknowledging your connection with the spirit of universal love, and it allows a sense of peace and love to flood your being. The tranquility that follows stays with you, reducing stress and promoting a state of creative awareness throughout the day.

Many artists have spoken of the creative state of being they achieve by quieting the mind and focusing attention through meditation. Just sitting quietly gives you a chance to go inside to ask your most important questions to you inner self. The composer Brahms, for example, wrote about his feeling of being a channel of creative energy during meditation:

> *I always contemplate my oneness with the creator before commencing to compose. This is the first step. I immediately feel vibrations that thrill my whole being. These are the spirit illuminating the soul power within and in the exalted state I see clearly what is obscure in my ordinary moods; then I feel capable of drawing inspiration from above . . . straightway the ideas flow in upon me and not only do I see distinct themes in my mind's eye, but they are clothed in the right forms, harmony and orchestration. Measure by measure the finished product is revealed to me when I am in those rare inspired moods.*

Our own creative energy is waiting to move through us once we get out of our own way. Cleansing the mind of negative thought, quieting the chatterer, and becoming one with the moment provides the environment for this energy to flow through us.

PROSPERITY PROFILE NO. 8

Linda Rettie, age 38, sailed a 33-foot Yamaha sail boat single-handedly for 52 days across the Pacific to Japan in 1981. She is the first American woman to sail the Pacific alone for so long a time.

Q: How would you define prosperity?

A: *For me, it's peace of mind and having a sense of self-fulfillment. This does not necessarily have anything to do with having another person in my life. I don't think other people add to or take away from my sense of peace. For me, knowing what I want to do, and having a direction, is my fulfillment.*

Q: What is your process for achieving your goals?

A: *I define my goals and lay out a plan of attack. I have to work through my plans, take my goals apart, put them into categories, and make a time plan for each part. This time frame is important; I need to decide the date and deadline for when I'm going to achieve each part.*

Once I have my plan organized, I let it go. I lose consciousness of my motives, why I'm doing each particular thing. That way I can concentrate solely on the tasks at hand.

Also, I learned the hard way to work 'as if' what I wanted was already true. For example, on my trip to Japan I needed a sponsor to make the trip possible. I did convince myself to organize, make plans, before I had a sponsor. But I had a mental block of fear that I wouldn't get one. I got depressed, which was very damaging and held me back. I had to work very hard just before the trip to make up for it. The mental approach to planning is of supreme importance. I never doubted, for example, that once I left I'd get there. That was very easy to visualize.

Q: Do you use visualizing your goals a lot?

A: *Definitely. I learned to fantasize as a young child. I remember our family doctor telling me something that has stuck with me through the years. He said, "People that can visualize themselves arriving before they leave home have fewer accidents." He meant it in broader terms and that's the way I took it. I always visualize myself there with my goals — having arrived in all things I want to achieve.*

Q: People applaud you a great deal for being brave and courageous. How do you feel about that?

A: *You have to break down bravery and courage. They aren't basic emotions. They are just symptoms. My single most important preparation was knowing and liking myself, because out there I was totally dependent upon myself. In sailing to Japan, I spent two weeks with no contact, and the rest of the time with no voice contact — only morse code.*

I also learned I didn't need others to feel good. I had come to terms with myself. I've always been an emotional person, and in the past, I let emotions dictate my actions. On the water, you can't. I had to learn mind control — to fight depression. All of my emotions continued their same mood swings as before, even though they were not being triggered by others. It was a great revelation to me that I was doing all that stuff to myself with my thoughts.

This mental work was important to me. I learned to separate what I was imagining from what was real. I couldn't lose my grip and start feeling sorry for myself. I needed every bit of mental preparation I had made.

I slept no more than an hour at a time, and a total of four hours a night. I was very much in tune with my environment and seemed to need no more sleep. I often had the sense of joy that comes with a heightened sense of awareness of all around me. I was literally on call 24 hours a day, but I never forgot the need for balance. I scheduled time just for myself — without regard for the boat — to relax. That is so important. I knew I'd build up resentment if I didn't take time for me — to read, listen to music, watch the sunset, whatever I wanted. I found myself obsessed with answering the question "Why?" Why was I there? There was no 'reasonable' answer. It was just a way that I could best express myself, and that's important to me.

Chapter 9

Consciousness of Prosperity

"Our life always expresses the result of our dominant thoughts."

—S. Kierkegaard

*P*rosperity requires that we know and follow the laws of prosperity.

We already know the profound effect that the discovery of physical laws has had on the development of modern life. The discoveries making civilization possible were as available to Neanderthal humans as they are to us. Stone age minds, however, were not ready to observe, understand, or apply the information available. The difference between then and now is primarily in the development of consciousness. It is this same growth in awareness that is now leading us to want to know the laws of *mental* manifestation.

In Part II you will be introduced to the laws of prosperity, which are tools to help you produce in physical form what you desire. These laws show you ways of releasing the potential of your creative mind. This 'creative mind' is the sum total of information from your physical, mental, emotional, and spiritual self. It is the source within you that unites you with the energy of the universe.

To fully utilize the laws of prosperity, you will want to view them as laws of consciousness. By changing our attitude through belief, expectation, and acceptance, we are really describing a change of consciousness about the so-called 'real world'.

What is real to you?

Most people will bang the table and say, "That's real! It's solid!" We can feel, taste, touch, smell it. But how solid is solid? Modern science has told us that in spite of how it appears, all mass is actually atomic particles in constant motion. These particles are vibrating and circulating with intense speed, reacting with each other in ceaseless, complex patterns. In breaking these whirling atoms down to their smallest dimension, scientists have found to their amazement that ultimately there are no 'building blocks' of mass — there is only energy. Fritjof Capra, physicist, speaking on the nature of matter, said:

> *The discovery that mass is nothing but a form of energy has forced us to modify our concept of a particle in an essential way. In modern physics, mass is no longer associated with a material substance, and hence particles are not seen as consisting of any basic 'stuff', but as bundles of energy.**

MANIFESTING ENERGY

The process of manifestation involves working with mental energy in such a way that mind has control over matter. If the reality of all mass, or matter, is that it is only energy, we will need to learn to work with energy to create a life of abundance. What can we deduce about the nature of this energy?

From astronomy and physics we know that all life, all matter, exists within the context of an infinite universe. Webster defines infinite as "having no limit in power, capacity, and knowledge; extending indefinitely; inconceivably great; inexhaustible." If our infinite universe consists only of energy, then this energy too, *has* to be infinite — powerful, beyond limit.

Understanding the inter-relationship between infinite energy and the power of the mind to create form is the most challenging and rewarding investigative study of this century. It will be through this study that we may

---

*Fritjof Capra, *Tao of Physics*, (Shambhala Publishing, Boulder, 1975, p. 202)

eventually be able to know how mind manifests. As of now, we can only observe that it indeed does, and make conjectures about how it does.

We have never had large scale, government-supported research in parapsychology, the study of the mind, such as that found in other countries — especially Russia. This is due primarily to lack of interest by science as a whole, and by lack of funds to support the effort.

Individuals from various disciplines, including Nobel laureates in the fields of physics, psychology, philosophy, and metaphysics, however, have been fascinated by the powers of the mind.

William James, Albert Einstein, Luther Burbank, Thomas Edison, Carl Jung, and others, have all actively engaged in some form of study of psychic interaction with matter. Generally, as they studied these interractions, they went through "a chronology of interest: first fascination, fear, or both; then avoidance of the phenomena as a distraction . . . and, finally, acceptance of them as natural, plausible, an extension of human creative powers, and evidence of the essential unity of all life."*

Marilyn Ferguson's book, *The Aquarian Conspiracy*, is an excellent resource of information on current serious, scientific inquiry into all aspects of the mind — biofeedback, ESP, intuition, right and left brain hemisphere differences, mind transference, and other creative powers. We are able to study some mind-matter interactions in a laboratory setting, but, as yet, much of the research being done on how the mind moves matter has proven somewhat inconclusive. Some of the research she reports, is highly exciting, however. For example:

> *Human intention has been shown to interact with matter at a distance, affecting the particles in a cloud*

---

*Marilyn Ferguson, *Aquarian Conspiracy*, (J.P. Tarcher, Los Angeles) p. 175

chamber, crystals, and the rate of radioactive decay.
    An intention to 'heal' has been demonstrated to alter
enzymes, hemoglobin values, and the hydrogen-oxygen
*bond in water . . . . ***

Scientists admit that "Every human intention that results in physical action is, in effect, mind over matter."†

Beyond individual, isolated, scientific experiments, one of the greatest boosts for the promotion of serious research on the power of the mind comes from the new quantum physics. Under the old Newtonian physics, it was thought that we lived in a mechanistic world which ran like a machine, with precise, predetermined clockwork action. Once it was proven that the act of observing changes that which is observed, we needed a new theory to explain reality.

Quantum physics provides for the phenomena of mind affecting matter. In this new physics, the universe is seen as a dynamic whole which always includes the observer in an essential way. It is a discipline that allows in mathematical language for the unpredictable — the effect on matter of the observing consciousness.

MATTER, TIME, SPACE, AND ONENESS

Since manifesting involves the *movement of matter through time and space,* we need to look for a moment at what we know about the interrelationships between these elements. In our universe, infinite energy takes the visible form of matter and non-matter. Matter has form and exists in space. Where there is no matter, there is no space, and vice versa.

We also know that *space* and *matter* are both required

Ibid., p. 175
†*Ibid.*, p. 175

for *time* to exist. *Time* is defined as that period required for one body to pass from one *point* to another. Without *'points* of reference', (i.e., matter) therefore, there can be no time. Where there is no space, there is no concept of distance, or of being separate. When there is no *time* or *space*, everything exists now, always and everywhere — infinitely.

INFINITE ONENESS

What does all this mean for manifesting with mind power? We have known for some time that *energy* and *matter* are *interchangeable. Nothing is ever lost or gained; it is only converted.* Therefore, when we see that matter and non-matter (without time or space and thus without separateness), are interchangeable aspects of the same energy, we begin to understand the infinite unity of space, matter and mind.

We are truly united in a conscious spirit that cannot be destroyed. We are at one with the universe. Wherever a part of this unity is, the whole is. Wherever we are, the universe is.

Therefore, at the energy level, that which we desire is already ours. According to Capra:

> The basic oneness of the universe is . . . one of the most important revelations of modern physics.
>
> In ordinary life, we are not aware of this unity of all things, but divide the world into separate objects and events. This division is, of course, useful and necessary to cope with our everyday environment, but it is not a fundamental feature of reality. . . .*

Some metaphysicians, in their study of the basic one-ness of mind and matter, have looked at everything we

*Fritjof Capra, *Tao of Physics*, (Shambhala Publishing, Boulder, 1975) p. 131

have manifested and have observed that mental intention *has* influenced matter. Looking for cause and effect, they feel we are in error if we give credit, exclusively, to the rational mind for these creative advancements. Rational thought, they say, is only the *channel* or connection with our real creative source: the subconscious.

Thomas Troward, metaphysician, scholar and close friend of the philosopher William James, felt that the nature of *infinite energy* is so much like the nature of our *subconscious* mind that they must be closely connected. He saw this connection as the magic key to the source of the powerful creative forces of the mind.

Troward observed that both infinite energy and the subconscious mind are subjective in nature. This means that they are both acted upon and never instigate action:

1. Neither has the power of decision making, so neither can *choose* to respond from persuasion or from a sense of right or wrong.
2. Neither operates from a personal preference — helping some and deliberately hurting others.
3. They both operate purely from cause and effect. In other words, all things being the same, a specific cause will always produce the same specific result.
4. They are both material from which other things are formed.

His conclusion then is that our subconscious mind represents a small part of the universal mind or infinite energy. *Our subconscious mind would therefore be our connection, our access, to the unlimited resources of the universe.**

As we recognize our oneness with all there is, we sense what is possible when we concentrate our energy on any one desired result. *If we are one, then we are not*

---

*See Thomas Troward, *Edinburgh Lectures* (Dodd, Mead & Co. 1909) *separate from that which we desire; it is already ours in thought form.* It is our creative thought power that brings it into physical form, because it is our thought energy in the subconscious that unites us with the subjective infinite energy.

By its very nature, *the power of infinite energy has to be drawing upon the energies of everything from everywhere at all time.* By willfully choosing to allow only positive thought-patterns to remain in our conscious minds, we are programming our subconscious to tune into this un-limited storehouse of infinite energy.

BRINGING THIS DOWN TO EARTH

For so long women have grown up thinking that if we were lucky we would find someone who would some-how tell us how to live. Some expert would give us the word on what we wanted, and on how to get it. We have thought we must plead for help either because we were helpless, or because we were worthy and *deserved* help.

Yet, it seems safe to assume that any laws governing infinite energy must be universal by nature, working without exception for all alike. This energy can only work within its subjective powers; making exception is beyond its scope, against its very nature. It follows, then, that it would be inappropriate for you to work with infinite energy with the attitude of needing to coax or persuade because you're worthy or needy.

This new approach suggests to you that you already have all you need within — that you are, *naturally*, con-nected with universal energy which is all there is. Your job, then, is to fully open your own channel, your own connection with this energy, knowing you *already* de-serve a fully rewarding life, and have everything you need to create it.

PROSPERITY PROFILE NO. 9

Janelle M. Barlow, Ph.D., Human Development Consultant.

Q: I know that you have built a really fine, financially successful business doing exactly what you enjoy most — giving seminars, speeches, and day-long workshops about maximizing potential. You also seem comfortable with your success. Has this always been true for you?

A: *I've always been highly competitive; I've always liked winning. It's never been a problem for me. I started early by winning a speech contest at age six. I liked the recognition that came with winning. All through school, it felt good when the teacher said, "Janelle got the highest score!"*

Every contest I entered, I worked hard at and did very well. I intended to win. Even today when I take up something I'm not very good at, like running, the image I see of me as a winner is strong enough that I still picture myself coming out ahead.

Q: You're not afraid of losing then?

A: *I do lose. But I don't dwell on it. I don't talk to others about my losses either — not even to my husband.*

Q: How about to yourself — what do you say to you?

A: *I'm aware of my losses and I constantly look for ways to change the outcome next time so I won't lose again.*

Q: In other words, you don't ignore the times you lose?

A: *No. I look for ways of turning the loss into information so I don't repeat it. That's the only logical and reasonable thing to do.*

I had a very important insight in high school that has influenced my life. Where I grew up, in the Midwest, the amount of money you had determined your place in the community. Financially, we were on the 'wrong side of the tracks'. Because I was competitive, however, I performed as well or better than others in everything I did. Yet, I always felt put down. It seemed as if everyone in the whole school put everybody down in as many subtle ways as they could. I protected myself from that barrage when I realized one day that there was a huge line of people outside my door — and everybody's door — just waiting to sling some negative criticism. I decided not to join that line.

Sometimes it was hard. It seemed as if that line went all the way down the street and around the corner. Everybody was in it. But it didn't matter — it struck me as stupid for me to get in that line as well.

Instead, I isolated myself and became a hard worker. I devoted myself to learning skills I really wanted to excel in. For example, besides getting top grades, working on the newspaper, and holding a job in high school, I would get up early to practice the piano for several hours. At graduation, I was asked to play my favorite piece at the senior recital. I played a great many pages of music I had memorized. When I finished, the principal announced to the senior class that when he heard me play, he realized he knew nothing of my talent, and wondered what other potential talents of everyone else in the class he was missing.

That statement has never left me. Ever since, I have been looking to see what I might be missing in terms of relating with other people. I look not only for what I might be missing in others, but in myself as well.

Q: When you are competing then, you are trying to be all that you can be, rather than focusing on beating others?

A: *That's correct — but I want to emphasize that the bigger I win, the more I like it. I want to win all the way.*

Q: And when you don't win?

A: *I never put myself down. I figure that if I put myself down for losing, then I've joined that line of people. It's everyone's choice — join that line or go for what you want.*

Part Two

Receiving

Getting what we want out of life requires that we be ready to receive what is naturally ours. Until now, we have focused on clearing the mind of attitudes that keep us from prosperity. We are now ready to use the mind for its highest potential — as a channel of connection with the source of prosperity — our creative imagination.

In Part II, we will learn how to put more of our potential to work with a 'concentrated mind action' process. The basic ideas of this process are not new. There are unlimited variations of these individual laws of prosperity found in almost every discipline. The truly successful have found and used portions of this path to prosperity throughout the ages.

What *is* new is that now these prosperity laws are combined in a step-by-step process that allows you to readily assimilate and apply them to everyday situations. By using new techniques with these old ideas in a concentrated mind action, their power is dramatically increased.

CONCENTRATED MIND ACTION

Nine Steps to Prosperity

GET READY:

Step 1 — **Law of Self-Awareness:** "When we know who we are and what we want, we can have what we want in life."

Step 2 — **Law of Wanting:** Experiencing choice means knowing what we want and why we want it."

Step 3 — **Law of Planning:** "Without planning there is no consistent prosperity."

GET SET:

Step 4 — **Law of Releasing:** "We must get rid of what we don't want, to make room for what we do want."

Step 5 — **Law of Compensation:** "There is a price for everything and we always pay."

GO:

Step 6 — **Law of Attraction:** "We attract what we are."

Step 7 — **Law of Visualization:** "We become what we imagine, positive or negative."

Step 8 — **Law of Affirmation:** "We become what we want to be by believing and affirming that we already are."

Step 9 — **Law of Loving:** "Whatever we want for ourselves, we must also desire for others."

Each step is built upon the results of the previous step. We experience true prosperity when all the laws are being followed. For this reason, read through the nine steps, then go back and start working on one step at a time. Incorporate the ideas your 'inner awareness' has revealed to you in the process of reading these laws. Don't expect however, to do everything all at once, or you may feel overwhelmed and give up. It is important to both see the whole process and to attempt just one step at a time.

Chapter 10

Self Awareness: Who Am I?

"They who are all things to their neighbors cease to be anything to themselves."

Norman Douglas

Prosperity Law No. 1: "When we know who we are and what we want, we can have what we want in life."

Did you ever, as a child, look in a mirror or sit on the side of a pool of water and look at your own reflection and wonder, "Who am I?" I remember one day standing in front of a three-way mirror in a neighbor's house when I was thirteen. I was fascinated that I could see so many sides of me by moving one mirror — or both. I looked so different depending on the angle.

My need to look at different aspects of myself didn't stop in adolescence. I soon found that what I wanted in life depended on how I defined myself. How I defined myself depended on how I looked at myself (a good example of this was my going through a period in which I thought I had to define myself as a 'strong' woman or a 'weak' woman). The answers I got to "Who am I?" were different as I grew older. I needed to continuously identify the new part of me that was growing and developing with new challenges.

Finding the answers to the questions, "Who am I?" and "What do I want?" is the hardest part in life. Getting what we want is a cinch after that — it's all down hill.

Learning who the 'I' is in the question, "Who Am I?", is what this chapter is all about.

The following approach to understanding yourself can be used at any age, and repeated, helps you keep a running profile on how you see yourself. We will look for the 'I' through our 'sub-personalities' vs. the 'inner self', and through ego vs. essence.

SUB-PERSONALITIES

One theory of personality, Psychosynthesis, indicates that we are not one 'I' but a complex of 'I's' — a collection of 'sub-personalities'.

Sub-personalities are different sides of us that have developed as a result of our interaction with the world in different capacities. As our roles, interests, and moods change, the way we respond to the environment changes. We are much different with the boss, for example, than we are with a new friend we've just met at a bar. We do not usually act the same with all our friends either. Every person brings out different aspects of us. In other words, the way we dress, act, and think, can change quite dramatically depending on the people we're with and the situations we're in.

Can you think of ways you are different with different people? Roles call for various responses from us and we play dozens of roles. What are some of the roles in your life — sweetheart, wife, mother, cook, sister, secretary, President? What position toward the world do you take in each role? What makes you happy in each role?

Other sub-personalities develop around dominant attitudes, moods, and feelings. For example, the 'Happy Helper' is continuously there to please, and will bend over backward to help anybody, anywhere, anytime. The 'Pessimist' remains so in the best of situations. The 'Judge' always has an improvement that could be made. If these and other sub-personalities are strong enough, they can dominate — no matter what role is being played.

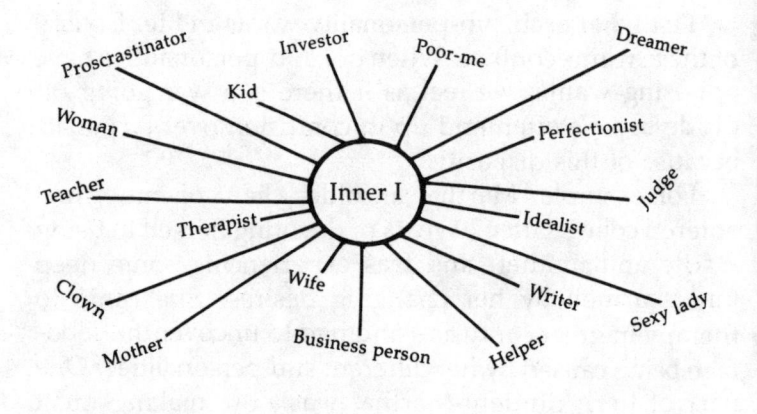

Sub-personalities are our roles we play, our main interests, and our ways of interacting with others. They often pass for being the real 'I'.

We all have a dozen or more sub-personalities and are operating in two or three at any given time. Each sub-personality wants something from us, and is offering something to us — all at once! In order to find peace and satisfaction in life, we need to identify our sub-personalities and discover what each one wants from us. Here's how:

1. Ask yourself the question "Who Am I?" twenty or thirty times. All your roles, attitudes, feelings, interests and ideas about yourself will emerge.
2. Write down your answers.
3. Categorize your answers by themes. In what way do your answers seem to be connected with each other? (For example some of my answers had to do with my concern for family, profession, health, love, security, fun, and strong feeling-states.)
4. Give your sub-personalities a name, and picture them in your mind.

List what each sub-personality wants in life. Do any of these wants conflict? When our sub-personalities have opposing wants, we feel as if there is a war going on inside us. We often end up in confusion over our goals because of this disparity.

For example, Martha, an older client of mine, had entered college after 20 years of devoting herself to being a wife and mother, and was experiencing some deep inner turmoil by her changing desires. She came to therapy in great confusion and had to uncover the sabotage being caused by her different sub-personalities. One part of her, 'Student-Martha' was now making great demands on her time. But 'Child-Martha' was getting pouty because she wanted more time to relax and enjoy life. Child-Martha undercut Student-Martha's efforts at every opportunity. Judge-Martha was always there — usually with derisive statements about responsibility to the family.

Wife-Martha', trying to play her multiple roles such as Sensuous Lady and Ms. Efficiency, was feeling stressful from lack of time and energy. 'Mother-Martha' was seeing her cherished role diminished as the children were now grown, and she required consolation and consideration about this sense of loss.

'Banker-Martha' was constantly warning that less time should be spent on schooling for the future and more time spent on earning money now. As these and other sub-personalities' voices were speaking nearly simultaneously, and each was demanding a great deal of attention, few needs were actually being met.

The value of identifying her sub-personalities in this manner was that Martha was able to stop blaming others for her anxiety, conflict, and pain and to see clearly that the real source of her upsets was inside herself. Her change in values and shift in priorities required some internal dialogue among her conflicting sub-personalities.

By pretending to place each one on a chair and to speak as that sub-personality, she was able to listen to what each wanted and to hear what each was contributing to her life. She saw then how she could compromise and give a little time to each and bring balance internally. The outside world was easy after that.

The object of looking at sub-personalities is not to become schizoid by seeing all the opposing parts, but to improve our ability as a conductor in charge of this orchestra of virtuosos. *We become victimized by putting too much energy into any one aspect of ourselves and over-identifying with any one part to the exclusion of others.*

While all sub-personalities do not need all they are demanding, if any one of them should feel starved for attention, she can become a real nuisance. Did you ever just have to go out for a candy bar or ice cream cone at midnight after a long, exhausting day? That's the child in you. Children will only be put off so long. With too many undernourished parts, we have a rebellion on our hands. Our peace is quickly gone, and our sense of prosperity has moved further away.

We need to bring balance to the demands of our sub-personalities, allowing ourselves to move forward toward a chosen goal. See the parts of yourself as an impartial observer would. Ask each part what she wants, and what she is giving. Prioritize their needs. Work toward a balance in meeting those needs by alloting some time and energy for each part. To get what you want in life with the minimum amount of inner opposition, make sure your major wants are satisfying the majority of your sub-personality needs.

'INNER SELF'

We developed each sub-personality as a way of expressing ourselves in the world. They are responses to environmental needs which are always changing. Another part of our 'I-ness' is unrelated to changing circumstances. This is our central 'I' or 'inner self' behind our sub-personalities. This 'I' is always quiet, always centered. As you still your chattering mind, you feel its calm, 'knowing' strength that speaks when you're ready to listen. Another way of looking at this inner 'I' is to see it as expressing your essence.

EGO VS. ESSENCE

The ego 'I' is who we *think* we are. We created it, and by its very nature, it is limited. When we are in our ego, we constantly judge and compare ourselves with others. We feel separate, out of touch with our oneness with the universe. We rarely feel satisfied, for the ego is greedy and there is never enough to feel full. In ego consciousness, our real wants are often hidden from us.

Ego is who we think we are; essence is who we *really* are. Essence is our true nature, that part of us that has never changed, is never fearful, never lost. The spirit of essence is like a tiny flame, mostly forgotten, but still determined to *be*.

Breathing life into this aspect of our self, we recognize that essence is our 'light' within — that soft voice of inner awareness that connects us with all there is. In this state of mind, we see we are a child of the universe, that we are already a miracle. When we are in touch with our essence, we do not have to prove anything to anyone, nor get permission or approval from anyone in order to be ourselves.

Our essence does not have a need for material possessions to be satisfied. It is complete in itself. In seeking to satisfy our essence, we are seeking our highest good. By limiting ourselves just to satisfying ego wants, we can become exhausted. Satisfying our essence can balance us and nourish us at a deep level. Anytime we express who we truly are, we are satisfying essence. Give yourself plenty of quiet time alone with nothing to do in order to get in touch with who you are. When we're in touch with our essence, *everything we do* is an expression of it — whether we're singing our heart out on stage or talking with a friend on the phone.

By acknowledging our inner essence, our real 'I', we feel closer to our spiritual nature. We know as long as our desires are life-affirming, and for the good of all, we deserve what we desire. With this freeing, prospering consciousness, we can go after what we want with a lighter heart, unattached to results. This allows us to handle another paradox in prospering: We need to *want* with a strong desire and at the same time *let go* of attachment to a particular outcome. Coming from our essence, we know our good fortune does not depend upon any one outcome.

Finding our peace, our center, our true 'I', is not always easy. We have layer upon layer of conflicting *shoulds* and *can'ts* covering that little flame and the wisdom it imparts. It can be reached, however, by a variety of paths, some of which are deliberate, such as yoga, breath and body work, therapy, dreamwork, and meditation.

Our centered 'I' is also sometimes reached in the most unexpected ways, such as quietly walking on the beach, making love, jogging, looking at the clouds. At such moments, we can temporarily transcend our ego, making possible that high moment of contact with our essence, where we know that everything is perfect in the universe, here and now.

To feel fully satisfied by our efforts, our wants must be based on an awareness of who that 'I' is that we're trying to satisfy — at the sub-personality and ego level, and at the level of essence. Only then can we best utilize our time and energy to get the most out of life. Finding out who we are is an exciting on-going process. To start with, reflect on these words:

> *We are not our feelings —*
> *   although we have feelings,*
> *We are not our bodies —*
> *   although we have bodies*
> *We are not our minds —*
> *   although we have minds*
> *We are a center of consciousness —*
> *   designed to be self-aware*

Chapter 11

What Do I Want? The Feeling Response

"There are three ingredients in the good life: Learning, earning, and yearning."

Christopher Morley

Prosperity Law No. 2: "Experiencing choice means knowing what we want and why we want it. Only then do we have the excitement and energy to go after our desires."

*B*ecky was 20 years old, and she was in love. More than anything in the world she wanted to go to Tahiti with her boyfriend and his parents. They were leaving in three months, and it would cost her $1,000 to go. She was in college, didn't have a job, and didn't have a nickel saved.

When she asked my advice, I suggested she write a letter to the Universe, stating exactly what she wanted, and how she wanted to receive it.

She wrote the following: *Dear Universe, Please send me $1,000 by June first. I need the deposit of $400 by May 1 to go to Tahiti. I really want to go. I want work in the afternoons at $4.00 an hour doing something I enjoy. I want to be able to study on the job too. Thank you. Love, Becky.*

Impossible? Maybe. Improbable? Surely. Yet, within 24 hours she had found an afternoon baby sitting job at $4.00 an hour, taking care of a two-year-old boy. His parents, both professionals, were willing to pay the unusually high price for Becky's enthusiasm and love for their son. Becky could also study during his nap time.

As the money accumulated, Becky paid her deposit on May 1, and saw she would have the $1,000 on time. She was concerned about telling the mother she was quitting; she knew they depended on her. When it came time to mention that next week would be her last, the mother interrupted her by saying she was pregnant and had decided to stay home after one week!

Becky's dream came true because she learned how to use the prosperity law of *wanting*. She dreamed the impossible and believed she could have it. Her experience gave her what many of us want — that feeling we can do or be whatever we want. Prosperity, as she found out, is the result of deliberate wanting and planning. Our ability to want is a magical gift. When we are excited and motivated to want, we are experiencing a sense of aliveness, and an inner awareness of unlimited opportunities about us. Planning puts a structure around that excitement to take us where we want to go.

IT IS OK TO WANT

We must sometimes give ourselves permission to want. We are created to want; it's natural. Wanting is how we grow. We are not selfish, bad, or greedy when we want — we are stretching to realize more of our potential.

At first glance this may appear to be the opposite of the Zen approach to self-fulfillment and peace of mind, which says the answer is to desire less. However, even those studying Zen are still intently desiring peace of mind. Emerson once remarked:

> . . . *the philosophers have laid the greatness of man in making his wants few, but will a man content himself with a hut and a handful of dried peas? He is born to be rich . . . . Wealth requires — besides the crust of bread and the roof — the freedom of the city, the freedom of the earth, travelling, machinery, the benefits of science, and fine arts, the best culture and the best company. He*

*is the rich man who can avail himself of all men's
faculties.* *

Fortunately, more women are availing themselves of
the good things in life by giving themselves permission
to desire better jobs, better pay, better health, more equal
relationships, more satisfying sex. The world is feeling
the effect of those desires, and as a result we are experiencing faster change than in any other peaceful re-
volution in the recorded history of womankind.

POWER OF WANTING

Wants are thoughts, and thought — as mind energy
— is creative power. When we become specific about
what we want, we are focusing the power of thought on
our desires. Focusing attention intensifies energy in the
same way a magnifying glass held over kindling will
intensify the sun's power to start a fire. The more specific
we are about our goals, the more intensely conscious we
become about reaching them, and the greater the force of
manifestation we create.

Studies have shown, however, that most of us have
not formulated precisely what we want. Our wants appear nebulous and difficult to put a finger on. It seems
easier to live with the vague sense that something is
missing, and to make do, rather than define what that
something is. One psychologist, Festinger, working in
'cognitive dissidence' research, has shown that when we
get what we *don't* want, we often start perceiving it as
what we *do* want, so as not to be miserable! There's no
way to know our real wants when we *pretend* we've got
what we want.

*Brooks Atkinson, ed., *Selected Writings of Ralph Waldo Emerson*, (Modern
  Library, N.Y., 1968) p. 696.

BARRIERS TO WANTING

Why is it we have so much reluctance to state specifically what we want in life?

There are a variety of reasons, but the root cause seems to be *fear of failure*. If we state what we want, then we're admitting we don't have it — and that feels like failing before we start. Other fears are:

> *"If I say what I want, and I don't get it, others will know it and I'll be embarrassed.... What's the use of deciding; I won't get it anyway.... If I name what I want, and I don't like it, I'm stuck with it."*

We can release these negative thoughts of failure once we understand the *beneficial* role of failing. Failure is part of the package of learning. When a baby is learning to walk, she falls. We wouldn't think of condemning her for falling. So, too, when we are learning to want, and to establish goals based on those wants, we need to keep our focus on success. Our goals are not set in concrete — they can always change. When our desires turn out to be not so desirous, we discard them and try again. Successful people know the importance of remaining flexible and of keeping their goals reflective of their feelings. They never lose sight of what they want, but when their plans fall through, they haven't failed. There is always more than one way to do anything we want to do.

Another major reason we have difficulty knowing what we want in life is that we have diluted our wants with 'shoulds'. As a child, when we knew what we wanted and said so, Mommy and Daddy, in their greater wisdom, assured us that we "really didn't want it, now did we?" We nodded our heads, and guessed we didn't. And something happened.

We learned to stop wanting. Since then, the whole structure of society has eagerly taken over where Mom,

Dad and the educational institutions stopped. We were told in school what was good for us, and therefore what to desire. Our entire commercial advertising and merchandising system feeds on developing and directing our wants. Under these pressures, we forgot how to think through wants for ourselves.

Defining our desires specifically sometimes seems to be an overwhelming task. One friend recently felt she would have to give up everything she was presently doing — quit her job, leave her marriage, leave town — before she would know what she wanted. This was too scary for her, so she did nothing.

One way out of this dilemma is to ask your inner-awareness to guide you in your goal-setting. Ask yourself: "What is my next step?" A step is not a leap. By taking one step at a time, we can try some things out, and *feel* if our goal is right.

GOALS AND VALUES

Do your goals reflect your values?

As we learn to utilize goal-setting to create desirable changes, we need to acknowledge our values. Wants which nourish are built on values we hold dear. These values, through our belief systems, are unconsciously determining our behavior patterns at every moment. Yet, few people can identify their values. Do you know what is important to you?

Look over the following quiz and let these questions stimulate you to think about values that are real for you. The origin of your values has long been unconscious, but just answering a few simple questions will quickly reveal personal preferences. Sharing answers with a friend is very helpful too, especially as you bring out details in your discussion.

Values — being self-reliant, daring, logical, loving, polite, tidy, congruent, truthful, honest, capable, forgiving, responsible, self-controlled, open-minded, and so on — are only *implied* in our answers. We must look between the lines. Our values emerge in our choice of work, how we relate to people, how we spend our time, how we think.

VALUES QUIZ

1. Answer these four questions off the top of your head:

   1. If you could do anything you wanted for one week, what would you do?
   2. What three things do you want people to remember about you?
   3. Finish this sentence: "Happiness is . . ."
   4. What always makes you angry?

2. What is important to you in your personal relations and life experiences? Rate these items on a scale of 1-10 (1 low, 10 being highly valued) and share with a friend *why* each is important:

   A loving relationship _____
   Being physically attractive _____
   A satisfying marriage _____
   Two months vacation a year _____
   A chance to be creative _____
   Making a difference in the world _____
   Freedom to make your own decisions _____
   A beautiful home _____
   Optimal health _____
   Unlimited travel _____
   Honesty with friends _____
   Sensuous sex life _____
   A large library of personal books _____
   Peace in the world _____
   To be treated fairly _____
   Confidence in yourself _____

Influence and power in your community _____
High spiritual experience _____
A satisfying religious faith _____
Dependable transportation _____
Someone who needs you _____
Someone to take care of you _____
Orderliness in your affairs _____
A close-knit family _____
Wealth _____
Other _____

_____
_____

3. What is important to you in your actual work conditions? (1-10)

To work alone _____
Regular hours and guaranteed pay _____
Totally unstructured work-day _____
Self-employment _____
Good supervision _____
Having a variety of tasks _____
Work in a small organization _____
Outdoor work _____
Opportunity for over-time _____
Little responsibility and risks _____
Short commute _____
Other (fill in) _____

_____
_____

4. Choose 3 things from the 14 choices below that give
   you the most satisfaction in your work.

   1. To be excited by what you're doing
   2. To help others solve problems
   3. To contribute to society with worthwhile work

4. To be recognized as an authority
5. To motivate yourself
6. To figure things out
7. To work within a structured situation
8. To think through new solutions
9. To have choice about time
10. To make a lot of money
11. To work in a team
12. To work out-of-doors
13. To be respected for your work
14. Other _____

5. Spranger's Study of Values says there are five principal personality values. Which ones do you mainly identify with?

Theoretical
These people have a principal interest in discovering truth without judgment. They mainly want to observe and reason.

Economic
These people value first what is useful and practical. They feel unapplied knowledge is a waste.

Aesthetic
These people take the most pleasure from the artistic episodes of life. They love form and harmony.

Social
The highest value for this personality is love of people.

Political
These people tend to desire influence, fame, and power first and foremost.

6. Name your five top values, based on your answers.

Over the next few months, observe if your desires change. Do these new desires reflect a change in values? Values change very slowly. Even though at the rational level we *decide* to be different, our automatic responses, based on old values, often lag behind. As your goals and values become more congruent, you become more powerful, for then you are not in conflict with yourself.

WHAT DO I WANT? TECHNIQUES

The closer we are to being the directors of our lives, the more in touch we feel with our dreams and desires. We need now to let go and daydream a little. It's very useful to establish a daily program of taking a few minutes to think, write, read, and meditate on goals. Some of these suggestions may help structure that time, which should be approached in an easy, relaxed manner:

1. List all the major areas of your life. What do you want in the area of love, home, work, play, health, finance, career, independence, travel, recreation, self-confidence building, personal growth, relationships?

2. Ask yourself questions and keep a diary of your answers:

   a. List what you don't want
   b. List what you 'should want' according to the significant people in your life.
   c. What hasn't lived yet in your life?
   d. What have you always wanted to do someday?
   e. What would you do if you could do anything you wanted for a year?

f. How much money would you like to be making in a year? In 5 years?

3. Daydream a little. Long-hidden wants sometimes reveal themselves in intuitive flashes. They rarely show you the whole plan, or lay out your way like the yellow brick road. Ideas come and go quickly in the form of images. Write them down. The dullest ink lasts longer than the sharpest memory.

4. Turn envious thoughts to positive use. When you feel envy at someone's good fortune, know that this may be a signal for some want you have. Release the envy and keep the desire.

5. Create an image of the ideal for yourself. Remember, it's good to desire; wanting is a prerequisite for receiving. How would you ideally have your life? Put on some soft music, lie back, and imagine an entire ideal day:

> Where would you be living? With whom?
> Where would you be working? Under what circumstances?
> How would you be playing? Loving? Being?
> Now open your eyes. How is your ideal different from your reality today? Keep a journal of your thoughts.

6. Learn to pick a bouquet of roses from the thorn bushes in your life. Inside every dissatisfaction is a want. When you're experiencing any negative emotion, keep asking yourself, "What do I want?" Avoid the inclination to just remain upset. Remind yourself that the world is yours for the asking — but you must know exactly what you want.

What you have been doing so far is creating prosperity goals in general terms. Before they become specific, they need to survive a series of other questions. Observe your intentions and reactions as you ask yourself:

Have I dared to think big enough?
Is my goal based on pure fantasy?
Is it achievable, believable, and measurable?
Is the goal life-producing?
Does it hurt any others?
Does this goal really belong to others?
Is it legal?
Is it good for all concerned?
Do I have the consciousness of having this goal?
Can I see myself already having it?
Have I investigated what I will need to do to have this goal (such as education, experience)?
Am I willing to undertake the undesirable aspects of the job?
Can I handle the rewards of geting this goal?
Am I willing to take on the responsibility of this goal?

At first, tell no one about your desires. Later, you may want feedback about how others see your project, but when you are initially building your confidence and accepting your own decisions as valuable, give your ideas time to germinate. Getting a negative response from others too soon might cause you to release it prematurely. You do not want to put yourself in a position of explaining or justifying your desires and ideas while they are still fresh and new to you. Let them develop strength of their own before you share them.

GOALS THAT CREATE

So far, we've been thinking about general goals, but definite results require definite ideas. For plans to succeed, we need to make our general goals concrete.

In defining a goal, we choose to focus energy in concentrated form on a certain event or thing. With this focus comes the strength and power to create what we want. We are now ready to go beyond the usual, "I want to be happy," or "I want someone to love me," and specify what would make us content, or what characteristics we'd like to find in a partner. We need to know precisely what we desire.

Wishing is only a start. As a vaguely conceived goal it will be vaguely expressed. The statement, "Wouldn't it be nice if . . . " shows little energy behind it. Wishes need to be made into declaratives in clear, concise words.

'Should-goals' are in the same category. Unless we're acting on our 'shoulds', they are only for show anyway. By repeating the thought, "I *should* write my mother every week," we can prove our good intentions, and still continue not to write mother. 'Shoulds' have little generative energy to change behavior. First you must become clear on what kind of communication you want with your mother and how often you want it. Your goal then comes from what *you* really want.

INTENSE DESIRES ARE CREATIVE DESIRES

Powerful, impelling goals that come true have the full force of the Self emerging from bondage. Expressing these desires brings a distinct bodily reaction — a "feeling response" that we can't miss. We've all had that experience of being extremely clear about some strong desire, and *knowing* it was ours long before it was actually manifested.

At such times, the world seems to be our oyster. We can literally see, smell, taste, touch success. We're not at all surprised when we succeed — it just seems natural.

A friend recently told me she 'knew' a certain job was hers when she received the call for an interview. She felt it was just a matter of showing up. She was right; she got the job that day.

Another young couple in Chicago recently made newspaper headlines when they won a large sum of money in a lottery. There had been no doubt at all about the rightness of their goal for them. They were in desperate straits financially, and had decided they had to win that lottery. They spent several hours each day meditating, intensely visualizing winning — what it would feel like when the phone rang, when the check arrived, depositing it and spending it. They reported later that it was almost anticlimactic to actually win it because they had already experienced even the joy of winning.

We have many levels of desires. By sorting through and finding out which ones are truly coming from our deepest well, we will tap into the energy we need to help create it physically. We don't have to force our minds to concentrate on something we deeply want and feel we deserve.

Take a moment and recreate a time when you experienced that power of 'knowing' deeply what you wanted, and got it. Take a deep breath, relax, and go back in memory to a time when you sensed something you really wanted was going to happen, although to all outward appearances there was no way to know it. Feel the 'knowing' in your body. Pay attention to the thoughts you were having. Remember the details of where you were, and what happened. Remember how you looked and felt. This 'feeling response', when you know your goal is on target, is your success signal.

When you have that 'feeling response', of winning, you know you have chosen your goal well. You are in alignment with your feelings, values, desires, and you have eliminated all negative opposition in your own thoughts. And a paradox now comes into play.

Our prosperity task is to be *specific* about our wants, goals, and plans to achieve our goals. What we are actually doing is programming our subconscious through the use of our conscious mind. We must be very concrete and list exactly what we want. At the same time that we are working with specifics, we must also stay aware that *our subconscious does not deal with specifics.* The subconscious responds to the *essence* of that which we desire.

So, while the subconscious must be programmed with exact detail, our higher intelligence, manifesting or producing through our subconscious, often does not bring about results exactly the way we think we want them. The end result may come about in ways we never dreamed possible. We've all heard miracle stories of chance meetings with a stranger who held the perfect answer for a pressing problem or need, such as Mary Ann in Chapter 1. We must stay alert to the possibilities constantly opening up around us from our source — infinite intelligence — in the form of creative ideas and situations.

There are few shortcuts to prosperity consciousness. It is only after we have defined what we want in definite terms that we become aware of all the possible ways of receiving what we desire. In that sense, prosperity consciousness can be seen as a process of *waking up.* We are responding to a 'higher self', that part of us that knows we deserve what we want. This helps to explain the paradox that while we must be specific, and desire our goal intensely, we must also let go of the idea of having to have the exact thing in the exact way we think it should happen.

Knowing what you want in life is a reward in itself. Spend as much time alone with your thoughts as possible, for this is internal work. No one can help you with your true desires. This is a wonderful game of consciousness and, played well, will result in attracting your life of abundance.

Chapter 12

Planning Your Success

"Becoming prosperous is first of all being truthful to ourselves."

Prosperity Law No. 3: "Without planning there is no consistent prosperity."

The three most important secrets of success are planning, planning, and planning! Once you have established over-all goals, you will want to establish plans for achieving your goals in all the important areas of your life: home, work, finances, recreation, and so on. Start by writing one specific goal that you want to achieve in five years for each major area. This helps you to look at the whole picture and see how the separate goals fit together. The object is to maintain balance in your life, and not get lopsided or carried away in any one interest.

FINANCIAL PLANNING

One major area women are awakening to is the need to plan for financial independence. You will need first to understand your financial situation today and determine how much you will need to fulfill your goals. According to some recent statistics, only two percent of U.S. citizens 65 years of age are financially independent; 23 percent still need to work; and 75 percent are dependent upon others (family, friends, welfare). In 1978 the National Council on Aging estimated that the total liquid assets per capita of all people 65 years of age (mostly women) was approximately $3,500.

A woman earning $15,000 a year for 30 years earns a total of almost half a million dollars. Unless she manages it well, however, she will end up with about as much as she started. *We need to learn to live on 90 percent of whatever we bring home.* Most of us do the opposite. As our income increases, so do our expenditures — or worse — we become heavily in debt for items of immediate consumption. Financial wizards tell us that the only good reason for borrowing money is to make money. Often the debts for consumer items last much longer then the items — either they've broken down, worn out, or we've gotten rid of them. Being in debt for items we have already consumed can be debilitating psychologically and we can end up feeling trapped financially.

Becoming prosperous is first of all being truthful to ourselves. It means taking responsibility for our financial state. To do this, you will need to list in a budget book all outstanding debts, monthly expenditures, and income. Next, list all assets and liabilities that are liquid and not liquid to give you a net worth picture. Establish a payment plan on your debts that will assure you a good credit rating. If you cannot pay fully, speak to your creditors and arrange a pay-back schedule you can afford. It may mean temporarily lowering your standard of living, and not buying those items you dearly want right now — but very quickly, a peace of mind and an excitement about future potential develops — and this peace cannot be bought.

What do you do with the 10 percent? That's the second golden rule of money: *Pay yourself first.* Skim 10 percent right off the top of your income to pay yourself. You deserve it. That is yours to keep. It is your investment money; envision it as your past labor that continues to work for you. You will want to invest that money safely and to continue to reinvest the interest it earns. Never plan on spending your original investment money. Have a separate account for savings to purchase your bigger items. This investment money is used only to accumulate interest and build your financial independence.

The truth is that no one has ever gotten wealthy from a salary. There are not enough hours in the day, or enough strength in the body to earn great wealth. Money invested safely with compound interest, however, never stops working. For example, $10,000 compounded at an annual rate of 25 percent with interest reinvested, adds up to over a million dollars in 21 years.*

A Prospering Woman must develop a consciousness of investing. We all know we need to earn money; we now need to learn what to do with it after we've earned it. It's not that hard. There are only a few areas we can invest in: savings, real-estate, stocks and bonds, precious metals, stones, and collectibles. You need to learn the risks and opportunities involved in each area. There are many free investment seminars to attend; some investment counselors will also provide the first hour free to discuss individual financial situations. Professional help is important, but all final decisions must be yours, for you are responsible for them.

The way we invest depends upon many things: how much money we need to live the way we desire; how long we want to work; our level of anxiety; and how much we're willing to risk to get what we want. Becoming money conscious is time-consuming, but so is work.

YOUR PLAN

For over-all life plans, ask yourself, "How do I want to be living five years from now? What needs to happen in four years to reach that five year plan? In three years? Two years?" Outline your goals in detail for next year. What can you do by next month? Next week? This week? Today?

---

*Mark O. Haroldsen, *How to Wake Up the Financial Genius Inside You* (Bantam Books, 1979) p. 172.

Be truthful and realistic in your planning. Establish a daily pattern of starting each day by reviewing your weekly goals and deciding one thing you can do every day toward achieving each goal. Remember that the whole idea of planning is to keep your mind focused in a positive way on where you are heading. It doesn't matter how big your steps are — what matters is that you take them.

PROSPERITY PROFILE NO. 10

Kit Cole, Cole Financial Group, Kentfield, Ca.

Q: Kit, how do you define prosperity?

A: *Prosperity to me means being able to set a goal and accomplish it. The more I set, the more I accomplish, and the easier I see it is to do.*

Q: You're in the financial investment business, so you must be excited by the idea of working with money. What changes did you have to go through in your own head that allowed you to deal freely with money? It has been my experience that women are not brought up to be prosperous. Do you agree?

A: *I agree completely. We were brought up under an ethic which has taught us to sublimate and put aside our thoughts about ourselves and support some other party. I got into business when I found myself with five children under six years old, and I had to make my own financial decisions. When I interviewed investment advisors for my own affairs, I realized that I was seeing only men and they didn't have a clue about the things that were going on in my mind when they were talking with* me. I realized that if I was having difficulty, so must a lot of other women. I was a second-grade teacher then and I changed careers. I went to a brokerage house and convinced the management that they needed a woman on their staff. That was 13 years ago, and there were no women at that time working as brokers.

Q: Many financial planners I've met just seem to repeat what the forms from the stock offerings advertise.

A: *What you see in business is what you see in life. There are a few creative people, and the rest are followers. Most planners still use the old Cotton Mather, Protestant ethic of 'live within your income'. The new wave of the future is to decide what you want to do, and then arrange your life to make that happen. This is so totally different, but so much more efficient than taking a blind shot and saying, "Oh, well, let's have 20 percent in bonds and 30 percent in stocks, two percent cash, and the rest we'll worry about." Our view is to decide what kind of return you have to get to live the kind of life you want to live, and that's what you do with your money.*

Q: How do you suggest women establish their goals?

A: *People should look at what they are doing and ask themselves if this is what they want to be doing the rest of their lives. If it isn't, then ask: "What do I want to be doing?" Much of the trauma women are experiencing now is suddenly realizing that all the things they are doing may not be what they want to be doing. I think we could avoid a lot of dramatic changes if we just keep asking ourselves this question all along.*

We have not been taught how to handle money at any time in our schooling. I recognized early on that we need a formula to come up with quantifiable goals. If you want to be independent in five years, you must ask yourself, "Given my lifestyle, how much does it cost me to live? What is it I want to do? How much will that cost me?" You then have concrete figures to shoot for.

You must quantify your needs. Go over the past 12 months and find out where every dollar went. That total is what it takes to make you independent. Let's say it was $20,000. Then, what are you not doing that you want to do? Going to school for an MBA? What does it cost? $4,000. Add that to the $20,000. You've got to look at what you want in life first, and rearrange the income, not the expenses.

Q: You hear so much about the difficulty in planning financially for the future because of interest and inflation fluctuations. What are your feelings about planning in these times when there is so much we don't know?

A: *The difficulty with that premise is that you never make a decision because there is no absolute certainty. You must take a look at the economic factors that you see, and you make some assumptions and act on those assumptions. And you always act. You always make a decision, and move towards a goal. If you find your assumptions are incorrect, you change your assumptions and make another decision. The biggest difficulty people have, not only in financial matters but in life, is that they are afraid to be wrong. If you make enough decisions, you'll be right more times than you're wrong, and you'll get what you want anyway.*

Q: What do you see as the Prospering Woman of the future when she does accept, in her own consciousness, that it's ok to be female and wealthy? Where do you see that we're going?

A: *I see that it's impossible to be prosperous and not be financially independent. Prosperity suggests that you have a level of personal security, and confidence. It's pretty hard to have confidence and security if you're hungry.*

Q: Or if you're depending upon someone else to feed you when you're capable of it yourself?

A: *Particularly so. We no longer have, and I'm not sure we ever did have, a support system where someone always takes care of the woman — the husband, family, or the court. The reality is that the price women paid for their care was always subjugation. When you marry for that reason, you earn every cent.*

Q: As you see it, what are the steps to achieve financial independence?

A: *Number one is to decide to be. Decide to make it happen. The rest is mechanical. You get what you envision. You must perceive yourself to be something before you can ever be that. When you 'see' your goal, not only will that help you make it happen, it will shorten the process. An example for me was wanting to travel. I've raised eight children and wanted to take them to Europe. The first thing I did was to book the trip. Most people think they should save the money, then they'll decide. It's faster to make the plan, then find the money for it.*

Goal planning has no respite, no relief. If you want to be financially successful, you can't retire from thinking. You must accept that you are accountable for your own fate. You can't rely on social security, or a pension, or on someone else. The important thing is to know that you can do whatever you need to, and you will do it.

You must also be willing to risk. Women have been raised to be adverse to risk. This is safe, but boring. You must be willing to put yourself on the line and be wrong. We too often decide that the man will risk — what we don't see is that the man then develops the skills, earning power, and confidence that is created in taking the risk. The non-risker just gets older.

We avoid risk because of fear. The most successful people in the world are fearful. The only difference between them and others who don't get what they want is that successful people just keep putting one foot in front of the other in spite of their fear.

Successful investment planning means sometimes making unpopular decisions, and having the ability to withstand criti-

cism. It means sometimes making personal sacrifices to bring about change in your life that will ultimately make you happier. Leaving the familiar is sometimes painful.

Being responsible for your investment plans may mean taking classes in accounting, taxation and basic economics so you know the rules, and see what other people perceive as what makes everything happen. That way you can assess world conditions for yourself and see if you agree with the recommendations of a counselor.

Most of all, for financial success, we need to demystify money. Money exists to make things happen — whatever you want to happen. So much of life is a function of the control and direction of money. The reason I'm attracted to the financial community is because this is where it's all happening. If you think about politics, programs, innovation — they're all made possible by adequate funding. We can work toward social change more through instituting financial practices than through the law.

Chapter 13

Releasing To Prosper

"If you want greater prosperity in your life, start forming a vacuum to receive it!"

Catherine Ponder

Prosperity Law No. 4: "We must get rid of what we don't want to make room for what we do want."

*E*very successful person knows and practices the law of release in some form or other. They know that to be prosperous, they must get rid of all they have outgrown, worn out, used up, by-passed, outlasted. When you have decided which ideas, relationships, beliefs, and situations no longer work for you, it is time to release them. Nothing stays new, shiny, or useful very long among dusty, old, cluttered, stored items.

The first area of release is with yourself. One way to stay open to the flow of life energy is to see yourself as a temple composed of body, mind, and spirit. Your body is your base, holding the structure together. Your mind is your communicator with your spirit, and your spirit is your connection with infinite energy. Keeping this temple open to receiving requires release in all three areas — spirit, mind, and body.

BODY CLEANSING

Health and balance in the body is necessary for any true prosperity. We have our own 'inner doctor' always available for consultation. You can do a 'Quickie' check-up by periodically asking yourself these questions:

1. Are you at the weight that makes you feel best?
2. Are you eating the fresh fruits, vegetables, and whole grains you need or are you primarily eating too many 'dead' processed foods?
3. Are you exercising daily: stretching for muscle tone and actively exercising for increased heart beat and circulation? We are moving creatures — it is almost impossible to remain in a depressed state while actively moving in a body made firm, flexible, and relaxed.
4. Can you relax? A tense muscle is a weak muscle. Muscles become strong by tensing *and* releasing. We are usually very good at tensing; all too often we don't know how to release in healthy ways. Alcohol and drugs will help to release tension temporarily, but the price is outrageous.

Give yourself permission to relax. Relaxing is not a sign of laziness; it is a sign of intelligence. When we tense and release, we are in step with the pulse of the universe. By fully letting go of tension in the muscles, we are making room for fresh new blood to bring nutrients to the entire system, thereby increasing our energy level and promoting greater productivity.

MIND CLEANSING

The most important release for the mind is letting go of negative thoughts. We all have these thoughts visiting us — but we are not stuck with them. Putting out the NO WELCOME sign doesn't work too well; they keep coming. What *does* work is to view negative thoughts as you would a flight of birds crossing your path. See them fly into view and continue on their way. Choose not to follow them with further attention.

We are only stuck with negative thoughts when we feed them by giving them our attention. Positive thinking alone doesn't work because we become emotionally attached to our negative thoughts. How do we 'let go' of negative attitudes (thoughts) when we don't *feel* positive?

It helps to remember that *thoughts come before feelings.* If you can stay aware enough, you can catch the thought that leads to feeling low. Check it out the next time you feel slightly down — what were you saying to yourself just before your spirit started its downward slide?

Becoming aware of, and dwelling upon negative thoughts are two different things. William James, the philosopher, had this to say on handling negative feelings:

> *To wrestle with a bad feeling only pins our attention on it, and keeps it still fastened in the mind: whereas, if we act as if from some better feelings, the old bad feeling soon folds its tent like an Arab, and silently steals away.* *

SPIRIT CLEANSING

When we cleanse the spirit, we renew our sense of universal harmony. It is an activity both refreshing and rewarding. Start each morning by giving yourself a gift of ten to fifteen minutes to be by yourself. The busier you are, the more important it is that you take this time.

Close your eyes and be aware of the newness of each day, and of who you are in the universe. Give thanks for your oneness with all there is. This process opens you to your prosperity consciousness, where you recognize that what you desire is already yours. By taking this consciousness into your daily activities, you make life an on-going cleansing and healing meditation.

---

*William James, "Gospel of Relaxation" (out-of-print pamphlet) p. 46.

FINISHING CYCLES

Once we start this cleansing motion of releasing body, mind and spirit, we will find it fun and easy because it is a circular action. The more we experience peace and order within, the more we demand it in our environment.

As we start today working toward having life more centered, focused, and peaceful, we will want to *clean up* the house, car, clothes, office, etc. We'll want to *clear out* all that is no longer useful, including old clothes, dishes, furniture, whatever; *straighten up* drawers, closets, garage, attic, storeroom, checkbook; *finish* the incomplete things in our lives. This may require taking care of those small jobs that are a constant irritant, running those errands, making those calls we've been putting off. It may mean deciding to repair or get rid of broken items. Unfinished cycles prevent us from experiencing peace, order, and harmony in our physical world.

This is also garbage can time for old ideas, beliefs, and relationships that are not working. Assumptions that are not bringing joy, such as "I *have* to cook every night" may be ready for the can. Develop the sense that you do what you do by *choice* — for that is the truth.

Worn out worries and doubts go, too. They only serve to hold you back, and get rancid when they've been around too long. Put all the old problems that wouldn't be 'solved' into that same garbage can — and release them, with love, letting go without further judgment or attachment.*

If the energy is gone in a relationship and neither of you is contributing to each other's growth, decide to tell the truth about why you are hanging on. Acting out of fear or lethargy is the opposite of moving creatively toward your joy.

---

*See Catherine Ponder, *Dynamic Laws of Prosperity*, Prentice-Hall.

RELEASING RESENTMENT

Another aspect of cleansing is learning to forgive yourself and others. One of the most important keys on your prosperity key chain is:

Prosperity Key No. 8

*Forgive all who have offended you —
not for them, but for yourself.*

We do not need to wait until others deserve our forgiveness, because we're not doing it for them. By holding resentments against others, we hurt ourselves more than anyone else. Clinging to our resentments is like taking poison every day. Why do we continue it?

Here's a little secret that may help you to give up resentments. Think about this: If a tiger were chasing you across the field hell-bent on eating you, would you be focusing on how much you were resenting having to run to safety? Probably not! Yet you would have every reason to. You are not at fault; something out there is doing it to you; you feel helpless; you have no choice. Why don't you resent it?

We only resent situations in which we know, deep down, we could have reacted differently, could have done something other than what we did. In other words, it is really *ourselves* and *our actions* (or lack of action) that we resent. We don't resent the tiger, because tigers will be tigers. We are doing all we can do, which is to get out of there. To forgive and let go of resentments, therefore, we need to ask ourselves what we could have done differently that we didn't do.

We can also learn to bless others — even our 'enemies'. Knowing there is a *lesson* in every problem, we can see that our opponent has just helped us to learn faster. It is to our advantage to forgive. We're not victimized saints; we're doing what's best for No. 1. The more we can forgive and bless with our good-will, the faster we are opening those channels to our prosperity. But it can't be phony. We have to *really* forgive — to recognize that the essence of the other person is the same as ours.

Sometimes you're not even aware of being unforgiving. Listen to yourself talk. Every time you hear resentment in your voice, know you've found someone or something else to put on your forgiveness list.

Asking our inner self who it is we need to forgive is helpful. *Forgiving our self and others is our single biggest step toward prosperity consciousness – exceeded only by the need to let go of negative thought.*

An excellent way to truly forgive is to (1) Imagine that you are speaking to the person who has offended you; (2) Ask her or him to forgive you for holding negative feelings about them; (3) Visualize that person surrounded in a white light that protects their well-being. If, however, you cannot find it in your heart to forgive, know that your inner self has already forgiven and you can tap into the strength of that forgiving spirit. A good statement to make while visualizing this is, "My inner self forgives you."

The warm feeling you receive in your own heart as your ability to love increases is reward in itself. But you will find that as you increase your loving responses to the world that you will also be miraculously effecting changes in the attitude of others toward you.

GIVING WITH LOVE

Another phase of the cleansing process is learning to give generously of your resources. *We must always give before we receive.* This is an old adage every successful business person knows and puts into action. Never pass up a chance to give.

This does not necessarily mean money. There is always something we can give, even if we are on the tightest of budgets. It may seem like an impossibility to give when our entire attention is on the need to receive, but it is expressly at those times when we feel needy that we will benefit the most from giving. Giving is simpler than we think — even a smile is worth a million to the right person at the right moment. We all have a variety of skills and talents that can contribute to others' well-being.

Feeling scarcity can be very depressing, and when our energy begins to spiral down into depression, our prosperity prospects spiral downward also. Our first task is to increase that energy level. One way is to give. It lifts our spirits to give. Being kind, considerate, and helpful toward others with our resources reminds us of our oneness with all of life. Giving also convinces our subconscious that we *already have more than we need*. We *are* prosperous, and expect to continue to be so.

The bottom line then, is that when we give, we benefit. It is time to give up the martyr role of giving as a sacrifice. Everything we do in life is for ourselves first. If another benefits from our good deeds — that's icing on the cake — nice, but of less importance. That's not being selfish; it's telling the truth. By acknowledging how much we receive by doing our 'good deeds', we free up the receiver of our gifts from any guilt. We need to thank others for the opportunity to give, because it makes us feel so good!

Prosperity Key No.9

Spend with the consciousness of giving with love.

Spending is giving also. When we spend with the right attitude, it is love in action. So much spending is associated with loss, and done with a grudge. We want to give with the same attitude we wish to receive from others — with love and good will. To do this, focus on all the benefits you receive for your money. Actually picture yourself in the center of a joyous network of giving and receiving with love and wisdom. This circular world of prospering energy is expressed in the song:

> *From you I receive*
> *To you I give*
> *Together we share*
> *And from this we live**

Let go of negative thoughts when you are spending money. Acknowledge to yourself the spiritual nature of money, and know that as you give, so you receive. Bless the money as a symbol of the unlimited supply of the universe. Tell yourself that *twice* that amount is now on its way to you.

By focusing your thoughts on prosperity instead of loss, you are convincing your subconscious that you are really serious about being prosperous. As a prosperous person your supply will always be replenished. When we assume the attitude and behavior of a prosperous person, we become one, through the action of the subconscious.

One bit of warning: Just giving and spending freely can make you broke fast. *Only when it is done with awareness does giving promote prosperity.* In other words, it's all part of the package — prosperity requires a balance of giving and receiving. Spending and giving must be done with a prosperity consciousness.

The law of releasing is often overlooked, yet it is the basis of being ready for all our good fortune that is on its way to us. What we already have is often obscured by living in clutter. If we do not continually put our house in

---

*© Nathan Segal, of the musical duo *Joseph and Nathan*, Mill Valley, Ca.

order, there is no space for anything new. When we feel our space clogged, *more* satisfies *less.*

Releasing, on the other hand, actually creates a vacuum — a space to breathe. We have a way to think clearly, see what is important, and plan for the next step. No vacuum remains empty long. This vacuum is no exception. It literally pulls our desired results to us.

PROSPERITY PROFILE NO. 11

Kay Cash Smith is an Organizational Development Consultant in San Francisco.

Q: There is a strong sense of achievement and personal power about you, Kay. My impression is that you've gone through a lot of changes to achieve a balance of power and receptivity. How did you start on your road to success?

A: *I have not always felt in balance. I decided at age 16 to be a lawyer and not have kids. I grew up feeling only what was male-oriented was validated. My mother's advice was to get an education so I wouldn't be stuck "in the female role." My father's message was that in order to be successful I would have to follow the male pattern.*

Q: What do you see as the male pattern?

A: *Male conditioning is to ask for what you want in life. Female conditioning is to wait for Prince Charming; wait to be chosen. The result in business is that men ask for a raise, and women put their nose to the grindstone and hope someone will notice.*

I knew that wasn't for me. It wasn't until I went to therapy that I found out that I had not wanted to be female most of my life. I had liked the trappings – the clothes, and power to manipulate with sexual attraction, but being female had meant, up until then, being weak, powerless, reactive.

Q: What changed your thinking about being female?

A: *When I chose to leave a great job in New York to follow my husband to San Francisco. I loved him, and wanted to be with him, but I was in great confusion about my role. Emotionally I fell apart. I found myself blaming him for all that was wrong in my world. The pieces of my life didn't fit anymore, and I knew I had to do something. I went into therapy and there learned how out of balance my male and female sides were.*

Being female to me has now come to mean that I am able to balance my nurturing, supporting, caring side, with being whole, capable, and assertive, and neither side operates at the expense of the other. As I see it, being male would mean the same thing. The only difference between the two is a certain energy that makes me glad I'm female.

Q: Has this balance brought changes in your work?

A: *I no longer need to manipulate to get what I want. My intention now is to create only win-win situations – not do battle. As I achieve clarity about who I am as a woman, my relationships with men are working better. It takes two to dance, and I no longer send out messages to the old dance. I can deal direct.*

I have need of my intuitive side to be a success in work. My 18 hour days would be impossible without the strength I get from what I call my inner awareness. I meditate regularly, using what I learned in India about "centering" to the higher self. When I travel I even carry my own incense to remind me of the environment in which I learned to reach that inner self.

Chapter 14

You Pay For What You Get

Material good has its tax, and if it came without desert or sweat, has no root in me, the next wind will blow it away.

Has a man gained who has received a hundred favors and rendered none? Always pay. If you are wise you will dread a prosperity which only loads you with more. He is great who confers the most benefits.

—Ralph Waldo Emerson

Prosperity Law No. 5: "There is a price for everything and we always pay."

While it is true that we continually receive abundantly from the universe, it is also true that there is no free lunch. What we often want to ignore is the tax that comes with the gifts. We pay for everything we receive in life, and that includes prosperity.

The gift and the price are more often called the law of cause and effect, out of which probably came the sage remark, "Be careful of what you want, you might get it." The reason for concern is legitimate. Whatever we receive has a multitude of effects. It is good to think through what those effects might be, and ask if the price is too high. For example, conditions around your job may be so unsatisfactory, you think you want out. Are you willing to pay the price of being out of work tomorrow to satisfy your desire to quit now?

We appreciate most what we have to pay for; and therefore the law of compensatory action really works to our advantage. Making payment for what we want jars us out of our waking sleep. When we realize the cost of our choices, we come alive for the moment to see what we have purchased. Identifying the price we will have to pay for each of our desires can actually help us promote our state of conscious alertness. We need to ask ourselves if we truly want our goals enough to pay the tax — for pay we will, in money, time, peace of mind, and so on. As we gradually accept that we *do* pay, we tend to choose our wants more wisely.

The law of compensation applies to all — it is a universal law. Yet it doesn't always seem to. When we observe dehumanizing, brutal, corrupt, or otherwise lawless acts going unpunished, we often ask ourselves if such acts, or individuals, are exempt from the law. We begin to doubt that a law of retribution exists.

But what we don't very often see is the cancerous effect on the insides of those individuals who gain at high cost to others. Human beings, by nature, are ethical beings. We pay where it counts most — in our guts — when we deviate from what we know to be right action. We never 'get away with' anything, because we cannot leave ourselves. We may try, with alcohol, drugs, etc., but we must always return. We are our own persecutors. The hell that rages within is a far greater punishment than any penalty which a court of law can inflict. The anger that is expressed outwardly is merely a reflection of the anger that is felt within at oneself.

Sometimes with time and distance, we are able to see the big picture, and observe the law of compensation at work. The best way to observe this is to be aware of how this works in your own life. We hear about those who have devoted their lives to others being the recipients of an outpouring of love when they least expected it. A friend of mine, for example, broke her leg and was given a Mercedes convertible with automatic shift, to drive for the duration of her convalescence by someone who appreciated her loving way of being.

Because the rectification of 'wrong action' is not always immediately obvious, however, many people have been sold on the idea that the 'bad' are successful and the good are miserable, but justice will be served in the hereafter. Ralph Waldo Emerson disagrees. He sees that the world balances itself perfectly.

> *Things refuse to be mismanaged long. Though no
> checks to a new evil appear, the checks exist. . . . All
> infractions of love and equity in our social relations are
> speedily punished. They are punished by fear . . . any
> departure from simplicity . . . or good for me that is not
> good for him, my neighbor feels the wrong; he shrinks
> from me as far as I have shrunk from him. . . . He
> indicates great wrongs which must be revised.*
>
> *Because of the dual constitution of things, in labor
> as in life there can be no cheating. The thief steals from
> himself. The swindler swindles himself.* *

In pursuit of our own prosperity, then, we need to
constantly stay aware of our intentions toward others.
Remember that the universal laws work on cause and
effect — impersonally. If our intentions are not good for
all concerned, all parties feel the negative effects. It is as if
there is a third silent partner to all our actions. We cannot
cheat others unnoticed, for we are creatures of integrity
and are always watching ourselves.

Fortunately, right action — action based on integrity
— works on this same principle of cause and effect. The
price of extending love, knowledge, beauty and wisdom
to others is that we receive more of the same for ourselves.

Sometimes we want to receive without giving, or
receive without earning. Material gain does not benefit
us if we have a 'grab all you can while the grabbing is
good, no matter who gets hurt' philosophy. As Prospering Women we must be in balance with the rest of the
world — receiving that which we desire and helping
others to benefit at the same time. If we continue to think

---

*R. W. Emerson, "Compensation," *Selected writings of Ralph Waldo Emerson,
ed.* (Brooks Atkinson, Modern Library, N.Y. 1968) p. 141

about what is possible, look for our lessons in both our positive and negative experiences, combine love with wisdom in our actions toward others, and intend good for all concerned, we can count on experiencing the best that life has to offer. The beauty of this law is in its positive effects; we become tomorrow ten-fold what we are today.

Chapter 15

Attracting Your Prosperity

"Be the qualities you want in your life and you'll attract more of the same to you."

Prosperity Law No. 6: "We attract what we are."

We don't need a crystal ball to know our future. We are attracting our future through our consciousness now. We are our consciousness, and the quality of thought we hold in our minds right now is attracting the quality of life we are heading toward. The law of attraction and the law of compensation are sister laws. In both cases, like attracts like — the quality of our energy attracts more of the same to us.

This attracting energy of our consciousness is expressed through our thoughts. Thought, with feeling, magnetizes. In order to be prosperous then, *we must first feel prosperous*. This reminds me of having to prime the old red pump when I lived on a farm as a child in Michigan. In order to get water on those cold winter mornings, we had to pour water down the pump first. On the days we hadn't saved any water to prime with, we melted snow to get it. So too, to increase our prosperity, we must start with what we've got.

And we have plenty. We all have enough to prime the pumps and start to feel prosperous. Our first appeal is to the conscious mind through an intellectual understanding of the importance of feeling positive about attracting our prosperity.

You do not have to be wealthy to feel prosperous. Prosperous feelings that radiate magnetic energy are not

generated by the amount of money in your pockets —
that feeling is beyond dollars and cents. Feeling prosperous comes from an inner glow — a sense that all is well in
the universe, that everything is just the way it should be.

Imagine living your life with a sensation of being fully
satisfied, and yet being open to the world. When we feel
prosperous, we know we can handle any turn of events
that might take place. We've got what it takes to live
freely without worry or fear. We feel a loving energy
when we both give and receive. With this valuable sense
of prosperity, we are more versatile, able to switch roles,
play different parts, and recognize life as the exciting
adventure it is — a game to be enjoyed.

There is no one thing that needs to happen, no obstacle to get by to start feeling prosperous. It is possible to
feel a touch of it this moment. All you need to do is close
your eyes, relax, breathe deeply, and remember a time
somewhere in your past when you were feeling on top of
your problems. We have all had those moments of knowing the love and support of the universe all around us.
Just by recalling those pleasant feelings, the chemistry of
your body changes, and you can achieve that prosperous
feeling temporarily.

While in this state of well-being, decide to mentally
radiate those qualities, now, that you desire to achieve in
your life. We do not need to wait until we have enough of
anything in order to be happy. If it is true that we attract
only what we are, then let's be all that we can be now.

Exactly how do we do that?

First, think through, clearly, what your concept is of a
truly prosperous woman. What qualities would she
have?

Second, list the characteristics you have now that you
like in yourself, and want to expand upon.

Third, list the kinds of people and situations that you

wish to attract to yourself as a Prospering Woman. What qualities would you have in those around you?

Fourth, close your eyes and imagine yourself being that Prospering Woman as you have defined her. Feel yourself having the qualities you believe she would have.

Begin to sense what being prosperous is like for you. How would you act? What would you do? How would you handle problems? What would you have? How would others act toward you? Really allow that exuberant feeling to encompass you. Open your eyes and list those things you can do today to express a feeling of prosperity.

RADIATE WHAT YOU DESIRE

At first, when we choose to radiate the qualities that we desire to bring into our lives, we feel as if we are pretending. In truth, however, we feel like actresses only because we have not allowed those qualities to emerge before. Remember that *at the core of our being, we are already perfect.* We are only moving one step closer to our true nature by deciding to express our higher qualities now. The deeper feelings will follow as you start attracting others with those same qualities and so feel reinforced from the outside by your efforts.

Keep in mind that feeling prosperous is enjoying fully what you already have. Right now all of us have resources we are not using, resources that can be appreciated now, rather than gathering dust waiting for that rainy day, or when company comes. It's time to treat ourselves like company.

Now is the time to utilize your best: give yourself the option of wearing your best — every day if you feel like it. Look like a million on an ordinary Wednesday afternoon, use your best dishes for breakfast, put candles and flowers on the table with the toasted cheese sandwiches. Dress in a manner that makes you feel not only 'appropriate', but *super*. Fashion ads tell us to buy their products for others' approval. Your own approval is worth a million times more. Many a salesperson knows the real benefit of looking good in a new suit is in how they feel *inside.* Looking our best keeps our spirits high. By coming from enthusiasm and a bright outlook, we attract success — whether it's in making a sale or meeting a new friend. We tend to see more of the opportunities around us, and, being 'up', we attract positive people to us.

LIVING AS AN ART FORM

Living prosperously is living life as an art form. All it takes is the intention of getting the most out of life in a loving, giving way. I had a personal experience of this while living in a student-housing village near a major West Coast college with 200 other veteran families. Most of us were earning less than minimum wage and supporting our families of three or four people, and yet a prosperous feeling predominated among us.

Many of these student-parents were working toward a goal they wanted and believed in, and the majority were pulling together in mutual support. Living so closely, we learned how to give each other privacy without having to avoid each other. We learned to care and help without intruding.

A community pre-school was established and run by the group, to perpetuate their highest values in education. Individual homes were artistically decorated from garage sales and miscellaneous want ads.

Many shared their skills in home-crafts: cabinetry, auto repair, pottery making, weaving, painting, etc. — all at very low cost to each other. Yards were not fenced and toys were often shared. Adults formed discussion groups on political issues and acted in concert for causes they felt were important.

Living there was a high experience, not from a prosperity feeling bought with dollars, but from the richness of living with a group of people whose mental attitude included the spirit of love and cooperation.

The secret to experiencing joy in life is loving what you have while you're working toward what you want.

PROSPERITY PROFILE NO. 12

Judy Hilsinger, a producer and director of news and talk shows in Washington, D.C. and New York for many years, is now President of Judy Hilsinger, Inc., a publicity/promotion firm with offices in San Francisco, Los Angeles and New York.

Q: Judy, how would you define prosperity, and do you consider yourself to be a Prospering Woman?

A: *I have never actually sat down and asked myself, "What is prosperity?" Success in itself has never been a goal for me. All I've ever wanted to do was have a lot of fun. When I do think of success, it is more with the concern that I achieve it without compromising myself and never at the expense of another person. What I really care about is having integrity and credibility in the market-place.*

Q: What kind of thinking, what attitude did you develop that allowed you to beome who you are?

A: *I was raised to be independent, aware that I must be responsible for myself at all times, and that I could achieve anything I wanted to do, if I just tried hard enough.*

Unlike some other women, I don't feel I am competing with men. I don't need to compete with others for anything in life for I'm the harshest judge of myself.

Also, I have partaken of almost every therapy from Gestalt to Rolfing (thank God I moved to California and was saved!) and obviously that has had some subtle impact in my actions. But then, I am always trying everything. I'd even try death if I thought I could come back and tell you about it five minutes later.

Q: Do you do any kind of mental work regularly so that you can achieve your goals faster and more efficiently?

A: *It has never occurred to me that there was a method involved in this game of success. I am optimistic though and that is a form of mental work that leads to positive end results. I am one who feeds off positive input and who tends to shuttle negative people right out of my life. Life is too short. I also look at creativity as something you bounce around, hopefully off someone whose brain is like a ping pong table – it becomes a dance and then a laugh-riot. It is never negative and it's so much fun. Creativity itself will not stand dissection and defies description.*

Early on in life I learned to use my brain as fast as I possibly could. Being speedier than others was a great defense, but it was not until I became thirty or so that I realized being right was not all it was knocked up to be. Being graceful and caring also has something to do with happiness.

Chapter 16

Picture Your Prosperity

"Creative visualization is magic in the truest and highest meaning of the word. It involves understanding and aligning yourself with the natural principles that govern the workings of our universe, and learning to use these principles in the most conscious and creative way."

Shakti Gawain

Prosperity Law No. 7: "We become what we imagine, positive or negative."

Real wealth has always been made through acting upon creative ideas. Millions of new thoughts are born every minute; only a few take root and grow. How fully developed the idea becomes is dependent upon the imaginative energy spent on that seed idea. The first nurturing action in our creative process then has to be on our own mental work.

Up until now we have focused primarily on the use of words — verbal and non-verbal — to do this work. Yet every productive achievement must first be imagined in the mind. Creative visualization — mentally picturing with emotion — is another important tool we have for mind action. By combining words with feelings and images, we can be more effective in programming the subconscious to manifest conditions that we desire.

Many people feel they have little ability to imagine, or cannot visualize. Visualizing, however, is a natural but often unconscious process of the mind. We could not execute a normal day's activities without our ability to create mental images, for all thinking is done in some kind of conceptual imagery. For example, every single plan we make, whether it is to reorganize a business, make a shopping list, or go to a movie, requires some sort of visualizing — perceiving in the eye of the mind that which is not yet visible to the physical eye.

Visualizing is also the natural process by which the mind communicates deeply buried feelings and beliefs. The importance of making this process conscious is that, without awareness, we usually choose to act according to the way we *envision* reality around us, not necessarily the way it actually is.

Much of our unconscious visualization comes in the form of fear images. For example, my daughter, Kathy, struggled with vivid 'pictures' of horrible catastrophic events befalling her new-born baby. When she realized these images were expressions of fears that had the potential of creating actual negative experiences she was able to focus on them in the light of rational expectations and let them go.

What we expect, believe, *and picture,* we usually get. Judging by all the negative expectations vividly portrayed in many of our conversations, it is amazing that we are able to create as much of the positive in our lives as we do. You can imagine what is possible once we have control of this power to create by deliberately visualizing ever more positive pictures.

The next step of concentrated mind action is choosing to do this very thing: to use this natural process of visualizing in a deliberate creative way to direct energy toward specific, positive purposes. When we consciously visualize, we are creating with picture-symbols — the language of the subconscious. We have greater access, therefore, to this powerhouse of manifesting energy. Picture-symbols, indirectly absorbed by the subconscious, represent not only our thought, but, used correctly, include information from all six senses — sight, sound, touch, smell, taste, and intuition.

VISUALIZING TECHNIQUES

The actual process of consciously creating imagery in the mind is much easier than you might guess. We all have an infinite capacity to produce bold, imaginative ideas and images in our own way. To prove to yourself that you can image at will, start with the easy stuff first. Relax a moment and close your eyes. Take a deep breath, see your favorite room at home. Walk all around it, touching objects, looking at the various colors in the room. Move a piece of furniture. Feel it under your hands.

What does the room smell like? Imagine yourself sitting in that room — how do you feel there? Try to get as total a picture as possible.

Next, let that scene go and imagine that you are holding a lemon in your right hand — a bright yellow, shiny lemon, about the size of your fist. Feel the rough texture of its skin. Smell it. Observe how it is shaped, with one end smaller than the other.

Now imagine cutting it in half. See a drop of juice pour out as you cut. Smell the pungent odor of the lemon. Take a bite out of one piece. Feel your mouth pucker. Spit the seeds out, and let yourself really taste the sour juice sliding down your throat. Now let that image go.

Imagine another scene — a happy time, a picnic, a time of a first love, a trip to the ocean — something you can easily recall visually with pleasure. Remember the details of that scene. Once again, look around you — what can you visually remember of that moment? Some people get more vivid 'pictures' than others. You may get only a feeling sensation at first, or even just gray or black scenes. Relax into whatever is happening; there is no right or wrong way. Letting go of the fear or worry that you can't visualize will often be enough to allow this natural phenomenon to occur.

Some people visualize best with their eyes open. Let your eyes go soft and gaze off into the distance, looking at nothing in particular, and allowing your memory to recall the pleasant scenes mentioned earlier. What feels good and works is right for you. Everyone visualizes differently.

Just having the *intention* and putting your *attention* on visualizing a scene is enough to focus the power of the mind.* Many people will immediately get some kind of picture sensations while recalling familiar scenes, even if they are very fuzzy at first. As you practice effective visualization, your ability to reproduce these scenes will increase proportionately.

To develop the ability to visualize, allow your eyes to outline objects several times during the day. Close your eyes, and see how much of the image you can retain. Repeat this often. Also, become more visually aware. Pay attention to color, design, shape, and the play of light and dark. Allow yourself to really look at details in plants, animals, nature, and people. Also try your hand at sketching to develop this 'inner seeing'.

Discipline is required to train our imaginations to focus on details of our desires until they are clearly visible to the mind's eye. It is as important as developing the discipline we needed to observe the mind for negative thoughts.

This discipline is easy, rewarding, and fun, especially contrasted with the rigid rules for success most of us were brought up with in our culture. We were led to believe that the only way we could get what we wanted in life was to strive with a set jaw, and grind away at some detestable hard work. The grinding approach to success goes along with the collective negative thinking in our society that we will only appreciate good after we have suffered; that being rejected strengthens character, and that we need to constantly whip up our will-power to achieve more and more.

As always, there is a drop of truth in everything. Sometimes we do appreciate good after suffering, we do

---

*Read Shakti Gawain's *Creative Visualization* (Whatever Publishing, 1979), on the ease of visualization.

get stronger with rejection, and we do achieve more by beating on ourselves.

It does not follow, however, that willful striving is the way it has to be. Constant struggling is unnatural, ineffective and inefficient.

ROLE OF WILL POWER

When we attempt to *force* change, rather than *allow* change with imaginative mind action, we are trying to use will-power in a way it is not meant to be used. Emile Coúe, early pioneer in hypnosis for self-improvement, confirmed that imagination will always win out over will in any conflict. It is not the true nature of the will to fight. The will, rightly used, clarifies our purpose and directs our actions to carry out the desires of the conscious mind. Using will-power to force our behavior or that of others to conform to the ideas of the ego is based on fear, insecurity and doubt. This is why resolutions using pure will-power don't work. When we try forcing our will from fear or doubt, we are bringing about the very thing we are trying to avoid.

Remember that *any* strong emotion, repeated often enough, programs the subconscious to create what we're thinking about. That includes *strong negative feelings.* Visual images caused by doubt, frustration, anger, worry — all negative emotions — hold back our good fortune and promote circumstances causing more frustration, anger, and worry.

Our only choice then is constant, careful, loving vigilance over the kind of program we set up in the subconscious with our current thoughts and mental images. By focusing on our desires, and on the pleasure our new patterns of life bring us, we are not fighting ourselves with our negatives. Our whole body is freed to move naturally in the direction we desire, attracting similar positive energy as we go along.

DIETING WITH IDEAL IMAGES

One example of the difference between *allowing* directed change and *forcing* change is in our approach to dieting. Diet by denial does not usually work on a long-term basis. What we resist, persists. When we lose weight solely by not eating what we desire to eat, our minds focus constantly on the foods we're not eating. We call forth the rebellious child within by restricting our 'goodies'. We are not free for a moment; we're only tightening the bonds holding us to the prohibited foods.

True, these bonds are stretched as the foods are held out of our reach, but as soon as the final pound of weight is lost, and attention to the diet is relaxed, is it any wonder that we literally 'spring back' to our original weight. We have not succeeded in moving on toward a new sense of being that includes being slim.

Visualizing allows us to experience how we want to be, act, dress, interact with others, feel, look, and generally how we want our new lifestyle to reflect a new inner feeling. When we practice being slim by visualizing it, the joy of seeing and feeling our slimness acts as a strong motivator keeping us there.

PICTURING YOUR GOALS

By creating a visualization notebook, you can learn to focus your imagination on many positive goal-images. Collect from various sources (old magazines, newspapers, greeting cards, etc.) symbols for what you want to create in your life. These can be in the form of pictures, sayings, statements, symbols of any kind that catch your attention. Some pictures seem to literally jump off the page at us — these are the kinds of pictures you want. Tear them out without judgment — you don't have to defend your choices. Once you have a collection of these pictures, you will begin to see symbols or themes in them representing wants and needs in your life.

By now, having done the work suggested in this book, you will have identified the major areas in your life that are important to you (i.e., home-life, love-life, career, etc.), and established goals in each of those major areas. Create a page in your notebook for each important area of your life. Choose one goal to visualize for each of these areas. While you are learning, choose goals you can easily see yourself already achieving, goals for which you have a lot of enthusiasm, and ones that you absolutely *expect* to have.

Create your visualization notebook of brightly-colored art paper. Choose colors that represent the qualities you want to bring into each area. For example, you might choose green for the financial page, and maybe rosy-pink for health, etc. Let the colors choose you — colors have a vibration of their own and actually have a subtle influence upon us. Label the goal of each page and paste an actual picture of you in the center.

Have fun and be as creative as you like with this notebook. On the financial page you may want to add some play money in large denominations. If any abstract images about goals come to you, draw them in your notebook. Sometimes drawing them with your non-dominant hand will help you overcome your own insecurity about your artistic ability. You will find gathering images and creating this notebook to be very enjoyable. Just in the act of doing it, your spirits will be uplifted.

The actual act of visualizing is most effective when done in a calm, easy manner, and with a positive frame of mind. For this reason, you will want to choose a time and place when you can be undisturbed. Allow your body to become relaxed, and clear your mind by letting go of all worry or anxiety, as well as all critical, judgmental thoughts. Try doing some simple stretches as a way to relax also.

Now, take deep abdominal breaths, letting your breath out in a slow, even, conscious stream, feeling more and more relaxed. Casually view the pictures you have cut out or drawn in your notebook. Lay them aside, and settle back. Pick a spot on the opposite wall on which to focus your full attention until your eyelids want to close. As you allow your eyelids to close, look up as if you were looking at the inside of your forehead. Pretend you are looking at the word "R E L A X" printed across the inside of your forehead for a few moments, then release your eyes to return to their more normal position and feel a wave of relaxation flood your body. Taking a deep breath with each number, count backward from ten to one. Feel even more relaxed with each breath exhaled.

Now recall the chosen goal for the day. Do not have more than one goal per day. When you find out how easy, pleasant, and effective programming the subconscious is, you will want to go inside with a shopping list, but resist the temptation. One goal per week works even better.

Allow images of achieving your given goal to form in your mind. Visualize each detail in a dream-like state, using all your six senses. Breathe deeply and ask yourself how it would feel if you had already achieved your goal. Stay in this pleasant picture until you see yourself acting successfully. Visualize an entire day being your ideal self.

In other words, you are pretending you have already achieved your desires, and you are already feeling the warm glow of success in your body. Your subconscious only does what it is told, and with this process you are directing it, telling it you want more of this good feeling in your life. It will automatically get to work bringing it to you.

There are two basic kinds of meditative states of mind, and you use both when you visualize. One is the *participatory, active state* where you are outlining, and picturing to yourself exactly what you desire. You will also want to stay in a relaxed, quiet mood long enough for your higher self to speak back to you. Remain quiet a moment to hear any messages you need to hear. That is the *receptive state*. Both are necessary for manifestation, for producing what you desire.

Always end by giving thanks to the universe for all that you have received in the past which has made your life full and rich. Give thanks, also, for this new gift which is now on its way to you, remembering that it must be 'beneficial for all concerned'.

Finish by counting up from one to ten, bringing yourself back to your normal, energetic frame of mind. With each number, repeat, "Every day, in every way, I am healthier and healthier," or "I am more alive, awake, alert, enthusiastic." Open your eyes feeling relaxed, refreshed, ready and able to do whatever is necessary on your part to take your next step.

Keep an on-going journal handy to record any insights and hunches that come up for you. Remember that creative ideas will come to you in 'flashes' only — rarely is an entire plan revealed at once. We must be ready at all times to catch these creative thoughts that will open our way to wealth, health, and happiness.

There are many benefits of visualization. The mind is projected through time and space, unlimited by what seem to be obvious barriers. It is exhilarating, expansive, and practical to boot. Visualization allows us to move from the depressive state of limitation to the prosperous feeling of "I can!" It takes time for the mind to accept rich mental pictures, however. Be gentle with yourself. There is plenty of time.

The next chapter, on affirmations, explains how 'statements of intention' contribute to the vortex of energy we are creating around us with our minds. It will be obvious how affirmations and visualizations go

hand-in-hand, forming the perfect marriage, an unbeat-
able team. Provided you have done your homework —
choosing your goals wisely and preparing to receive all
the good that is ready to flow to you — you will now be
able to create miracle after miracle in your life and in the
lives of those around you.

Chapter 17

Declare Your Prosperity

"Speak to yourself as if what you desire is already true and it already is."

Prosperity Law No. 8: "We become what we want to be by believing and affirming that we already are."

*A*n *affirmation* is a positive thought held with conviction to produce a desired result. Effective affirmation is the act of stating positively in written and oral form that which is yet to be. It is an act of courage on the spiritual level, for it is a positive thought form in the face of an unknown situation.

As you recall from earlier chapters, any thought held long enough with intense feelings in the conscious mind will impress itself upon the subconscious. Sufficiently impressed, the subconscious then has no choice but to create for us what we desire.

Affirming by statement is a natural method of manifestation that we have been unconsciously using all along. Each of the 50,000 thoughts we have each day is actually an affirmation — positive or negative — and each is bringing about change in our lives, accordingly. We don't have a choice of programming or not programming the subconscious. As long as we are thinking, we are doing it. We need to be aware of *what* we are programming! We want to assertively program positive thoughts so that we reap positive results.

Affirming is not the same as wishing. Wishing actually confirms doubt that this goal can happen. It is a passive expression of our desire. To affirm, on the other hand, is to *make firm* — to declare assertively that it is so. We are saying 'yes' to our goal by affirming, rather than saying a wishful maybe.

The act of affirming that what we want is ours makes sense when we define our true nature as creative beings, and our true role in life as achieving an expanded awareness. We live in a supportive universe, overflowing with beautiful gifts. We are affirming only what is rightfully ours.

When you are just learning to affirm, it will be easier to maintain focus and develop skill in this technique if you choose goals that are well defined, truly desired, and that have enthusiastic energy behind them.

Vaguely conceived or vaguely worded goals leave us open to the cosmic humor. For example, at a recent prosperity conference, one woman related a story of her first attempt at affirmation. She had been a widow for some time. She decided to bring a man into her life, as she was lonely. Consequently she had been affirming "I want a man in the house." She did this for about a week. She got her desire all right, but not in the way she had intended. One day she walked into her house to find a burglar in the kitchen! She saw her error, and changed her affirmation to be more specific: "I want a man to love, who loves me and lives with me." She finally got what she really wanted and now has a loving relationship to come home to.

Affirmations and visualizations go hand in hand. You will want to choose and declare a goal through an affirmation that you can 'see' yourself already having. You must hold in consciousness a $30,000-a-year job before you can effectively draw one from the universal warehouse. You must be able to *see* and *feel* yourself driving the car of your dreams, having the good relationship, or creating the corporate structure before you can attract them into your life on any permanent basis.

TECHNIQUES OF AFFIRMING

The process for stating an affirmation and following through is simple:

Write it:
1. State your desire specifically and intensely: "I now weigh 120 pounds, my ideal weight."
   Not: "I want to look somewhat better than I do."
2. State it in a positive, active way: "I am now losing one pound a day."
   Not: "I am no longer fat."
3. State it as if it is already true: "I am losing weight now."
   Not: "I will be losing weight."
4. State it in a few words and to the point: "I now weigh 120 pounds."
   Not: "I now weigh about the right amount and I hope to lose all extra weight because I'm not eating cookies in the future."

Use it:
1. Twice a day, repeat your affirmations out loud, five times each. Say it with enthusiasm, experiencing the joy of having received what you want.
2. Write your affirmations ten times each day with full attention and intention of receiving your goal.
3. Carry your affirmations with you on 3-by-5 cards to read from time to time. As you read, visualize yourself having achieved your desires.

It is basically that simple. To assure that you get the most from your affirmations, you may want to consider the following points:

1. Only thoughts with intense feeling bring results. You will want to repeat your affirmations until you *feel* you have achieved your desires.

2. Repeat your affirmations in private. Our affirmations are our secret. We want to prove this process to ourselves, and distracting energies dilute our focus and intention.

3. Choose a time that's right for you. For many people, the best time of the day for writing or reading affirmations is upon rising in the morning and just before sleeping. Another effective time for repeating affirmations is while doing anything in a rote manner, such as long distance highway driving. In both cases, we are usually in a more semi-hypnotic, relaxed state, and so have greater access to our subconscious.

When we relax in a receptive, passive mood, our brain waves dip frequently into the slower 'alpha' wave, or meditative pattern. At these times we are more open to suggestion on the deeper levels of consciousness.

The state of mind with which we approach every step of concentrated mind action is very important. It is especially so in the visualizing and affirming steps. These two steps work well only when we are in a positive, expectant, trusting mood. At such times we feel full, connected to our source, and our personal power is at our command.

Negative states tend to destroy any good we try to start. Feelings of anger, resentment, fear, doubt, boredom interfere with our positive programming. It seems best at these times to deliberately focus on the negative problem to *define* it, and to *deal* with it to the best of your ability. Define who did what to whom; what needs to happen that hasn't been done; and what you can do about the situation. Always look for the message in the negative: what is there for you to learn in this situation?

When you have done all you can do about a negative situation, it is time to release it. One characteristic of winners is that they know when and how to release a problem, knowing their subconscious will continue to work on it and later produce the perfect answer. The quickest way to release is to return the focus of your attention to lifting your spirits. You can do this with exercise, breathing deeply, taking time to read inspiring words — whatever works to get your energies flowing in a positive way.

Pay attention to all negative thoughts which are contradicting specific affirmations. These are important messages, for they point out our blocks — ways we are keeping ourselves back. Write them down and look for themes behind the objections. For example if you now weigh 180 pounds and your goal is 120 pounds, you may start affirming:

Affirmation	Objections
"I now weigh 120 pounds."	Oh yeah! With all that crap you eat. You're lucky that you don't weigh 220 pounds.
"I now weigh 120 pounds."	Not with that candy and goodies at the office
"I now weigh 120 pounds."	You can't resist free food and you have a lot of social luncheons to attend.

In light of these negatives, you may want to modify your affirmations to be more realistic. Your negative statements may be telling you that you are not ready for your ideal desire yet. You may want to adjust your goals to bring change in incremental steps. For example if you find it easier to accept your ability to be 150 pounds, start by affirming "I now weigh 150 pounds."

Affirmation and visualization are part of the natural process of manifestation that we have been using unconsciously. To develop skill at using them consciously will require dedication, commitment, and patience. Never push; there *is* time. Pushing doesn't work anyway. What we are learning to do is to relax into beneficial change the natural way. We all want everything yesterday, but the universe has its own time schedule. We didn't get into our present situation overnight. By knowing that our good fortune is coming, it is easier to develop patience.

The most effective affirmations are those you create for yourself, based specifically on your goals. Here are a few that clients of mine have found helpful:

I am at peace with nature
All I have is now
This problem is only an obstacle to overcome
My self-worth is located within
I am an equal part of all humanity and life
I dress to please myself
I admit my mistakes easily
I like to be alone; my privacy is important
All heroes are people, equal to myself
I accept myself physically
I approve of myself
I welcome challenges
I am responsible for my good health
I have all the time I need
I am willing to receive
I deserve all the good that is coming to me
My wealth is in my mind
I now forgive everyone for every offense
I bless my money, and each dollar I spend or give is
   returned multiplied
I give myself and others the right to say no
I am always in the right place at the right time

The more positive thoughts I have, the more positive my life is

I am rich, I am free, easily and effortlessly

ACTING 'AS IF'

Effective affirmation accompanied by acts of conviction impress the subconscious. We need to actively prepare to receive by acting 'as if' what we want is on its way.
We want to act 'as if' we are already thin, beautiful,
smart, wealthy, healthy. We do this by using all the resources we have now. In this way, we are incorporating
the law of attraction. If a trip is your goal, make out your
packing list and get brochures from the travel agent. Buy
that dress a size too small knowing that is what you will
wear. Have your outfit planned for that job interview you
want.

When we affirm and visualize, we are working with
energies that by-pass reason, forced will, and judgment
of the conscious mind. We are working directly with the
energy of the subconscious, which is subjective and
non-judgmental. To allow the process of affirmation to
work, therefore, you need to affirm the belief that reprogramming the subconscious works.

Some people have difficulty stating that their affirmation is already true. However, there is no incongruency
here. As you visualize and affirm, your goal *does* already
exist — in the form of an idea. Remember that nothing
was ever created that did not first exist as an idea. The
idea, then, is your goal in embryonic form. Therefore,
you tell the truth when you affirm your desire as already
happening.

By coupling affirmation and visualization with your
positive action, you are insuring the full unfolding of
your goal in physical reality.

Chapter 18

Love Your Way To Prosperity

"Peace of mind comes from not wanting to change others."

Gerald Jampolsky

Prosperity Law No. 9: "Whatever we want for ourselves, we must also desire for others."

*I*f we are to prosper individually, we must see ourselves contributing to others — caring for, supporting, and encouraging them. True prosperity comes from responsible, 'right' relationships with others.

Religious doctrine and metaphysical teaching have told us that it never works to attack, make others wrong, or win at another's expense. A commonly accepted cultural ideal of right living in western civilization is to turn the other cheek when offended. This action is based on an ideal of self-sacrifice and an altruistic concern for others. Once we understand, however, that 'right living is also self-serving, prosperous living, we may be motivated to move even more rapidly and effortlessly toward that ideal.

This prosperity law of loving action is really a statement about who we are within our context: we are each part of a delicately woven whole. Just as every living cell is a self-contained, self-satisfying world, yet interdependent upon many others, so we too are autonomous, self-willed, creative beings — yet one within a whole.

We all want to win at the game of life. The emerging real truth is that the best way to do this is for us to love and promote the best in each other — not for self-sacrificing reasons, but for the most powerfully motivating factor on earth: self-interest. When we catch on and play the game consciously, we *all* win.

The importance of this law is seen and felt in our global relations with one another. It is easy to feel helpless and defeated in the face of world problems — yet the same laws of prosperity apply as much to a culture as they do to the individual. What we do individually is a microcosm of what we as a society do. Our individual thoughts act in synergy to form a mass consensus —a subconscious idea that we reproduce in physical reality. Since our cultural consensus is a reflection of our individual thoughts and actions, we need to look inwardly at the direction of our thoughts. Globally, it is obvious that what we need is drastic revision in the way we are using mind action.

Almost every situation in today's world is forcing us to seek a solution of balance. The problems of ecology and pollution are good examples. We are all on planet earth together — there is no escape. So our only choice is playing the game of life from a 'win-win' or a 'lose-lose' position.

The time is over for thinking that our problems would be solved if only one group or another would cease to be a threat. The consumer *is* the producer when it comes to environmental issues. The lines between capital and labor blur as each learns they must cooperate to avoid economic collapse when faced with the threat of depression. We see the broader view of our problems if we begin to ask how we can continue to produce without polluting the environment. How can we defend without annihilating each other? How can we build without obliterating that which we already have?

How do we face these and other social issues, utilizing mind action to prosper as an individual, as a nation, and as a world?

We can start with our own individual thought, for that is where the movement of all mass thought starts.

Our mass consensus is created out of our individual consciousness. Each of us does make a difference.

This has not always been obvious. The pragmatists among us saw no ultimate social value in the personal growth movement of the 60's and 70's. Efforts to increase individual consciousness through awareness of body and feeling states was seen as 'contemplating one's navel' — useless self indulgence. Critics of this movement feared excessive attention on self would destroy concern for others and inhibit the work of the world. They argued that if we drew attention away from the problems of society in favor of increasing attention to self-awareness of inner wants and needs, we would become a nation of self-righteous hedonists. They pointed with alarm at boastful, self-centered personalities as prime examples of what happens with so-called 'self-love' taken to the extreme.

The attitudes of these critics demonstrate the pitfalls of either/or thinking. We are creatures who need to pay attention to *both* our inner and outer worlds. Egotistical attitudes are not the result of increased self-love and self-confidence, but demonstrate the lack of any *real* self-esteem. When we feel good about ourselves there is no need to boast and bluster.

Our inner work supports our outer work. We must go 'inside' to contact our higher self for regeneration, self-approval, and self-direction. For that knowledge to be of real value, however, we must express it in the world as creative, loving action helping human kind.

Far from being useless, spending time, money and energy on one's own self-awareness is the only firm foundation for ultimate solutions to world problems. Guns and bombs create temporary 'solutions' which lead to ever bigger problems. Becoming self-aware is a process of changing attitudes — of becoming more fully human. Webster defines 'human' as: "Creatures able to understand, evaluate, choose and accept responsibility."

The more fully human we are, the more we can understand the condition of our 'oneness'. The more we see through the peripheral actions to the essence of each other, the more loving we can be. We come to realize that no one has ever done anything that we haven't at least thought of at one time in our life. We therefore learn to forgive — the highest human faculty we have.

Exploitive action comes from the mass thought that there is not enough — love, money, sex, energy, power, land, water, food, time, health, opportunity. Yet there *is no shortage* of any of these. We have plenty of everything we need to be happy. The only barriers to abundance are our beliefs about the inevitability of scarcity.

An example of the abundance in which we live is obvious in a quote from a recent "World Hunger Action-letter," published by the American Friends Service Committee. They reported that $17 billion a year is the estimated cost of providing adequate food, water, education, health care, and housing for all the world's residents. This is about the same amount the world spends for arms — every two weeks."[*]

In spite of all evidence to the contrary, we somehow have come to believe that poverty and starvation are just a natural part of life. Yet we have attained all the know-how we need to feed the world's population. We are now beginning to overcome that belief system with the help of several influencial organizations such as Unicef, The Hunger Project, and the American Friends Service Committee.

Ask yourself what beliefs you hold about scarcity in your life. Make a list of everything that seems to be a scarce commodity.

Almost everyone feels there is not enough *time*; yet there are still twenty-four hours each day — the same as always. It is only our thoughts about structuring time

---

[*]As reported in Ms. Magazine, August, 1981.

that give us the impression of abundance or scarcity.

Many yearn for *love* and feel there is not enough of it in the world. I've heard many women and men express the feeling that there aren't many good people around to choose from. There are *plenty* of wonderful people — both men and women — wanting to give and receive love. Love exists in our minds. We limit ourselves only because of our shields of fear, our shields against love.

We hear so much about the *energy* crisis. The only crisis we are facing is the challenge to create new forms of energy to use as our fossil fuel is burning up. All that exists in the universe is energy. There is no lack of energy, only lack of commitment to find new sources. For example, the United States government, is spending more money on their military marching bands than they are on solar, wind, and other alternative sources of energy.

Water itself is not scarce. Clean water is scarce. How we decide to use the bountiful supply of water we have is what determines its purity. Those decisions are dependent upon our consciousness.

Then there's *money*. We own the bank that supplies our wealth. It is the natural flow of our creative energy that overflows into money. When we are living a loving, giving life, fully conscious of who we are and what we want, we have the ability to obtain all the money we need through our creative ideas.

By observing, without a belief system of scarcity, we see that our universe isn't skimpy. We are oversupplied in great abundance — with love.

Coming from a new consciousness of abundance, we learn that winning is an attitude and happiness is a decision. We can release and relax into our prosperity when we know, affirm, visualize, and experience the love of the universe through the abundance that surrounds us. By expressing love for each other we are only paying back a little of that which we have already received.

Chapter 19

Prosperity Tune-up

Now that you've read this far, and done the work, you are ready to reap your rewards. I'm sure your life has already been changing in many ways as you incorporate the prosperity principles. To promote your prosperity even more, you may want to review the following "Prosperity Consciousness Tune-up" questions from time to time. This may help you get in touch with ways you are still holding back from your full prosperity.

Keep in your consciousness the idea that only *thought* stands between you and what you desire. By changing your consciousness, you change your world. Where your mind goes, creative energy flows.

PROSPERITY TUNE-UP CHECK LIST

1. How well do I know myself and what I want? Until we know who we are, we can't know what we want.

2. Do I really want to succeed? How much? We only get what we want deep down.

3. Have I developed a strong power of concentration — an ability to focus on one thing at a time? Scattered desires create scattered results.

4. Do I basically feel that I have choice in life? To take responsibility is to recognize choice in attitude.

5. Do I feel life is pretty much okay the way it is? We have to start from where we are — that means accepting first what is now.

6. Do I know my basic purpose in life? Once we know the answer to this, it's much easier to know the answers to our other questions.

7. Am I willing to take calculated risks to get what I want? We'll never know enough. At one point, we have to be willing to jump into the unknown armed only with our intuitive feelings.

8. Am I comfortable spending, receiving, saving and investing money? Money is our helpful ally.

9. Do I feel like a complete, whole person even if I happen to be temporarily without a partner in my life?

10. Given my talents, do I know what the universe might expect from me? What does the world need that can best be done by me?

11. Have I cleared a space for success in my life? Some people are still giving energy to things that happened five, ten, fifteen years ago. We need to release situations, people, and things to make room for the new.

12. Have I forgiven everyone I need to forgive? Holding resentments takes both hands. To reach out for the love, joy, and success in all ways of life, we want to free ourselves of the burden of resentment — not for the sake of the other, but for ourselves!

13. Have I reconciled my conflicting desires? Is one part of me holding back what another part wants? Am I listening to both sides? Remember that the power of suppressed desires sabotages those desires we're going after.

14. Am I specific in my direction? Every good ship's captain knows her course before taking her ship to sea. You will only know when you get there *if* you know where you're going.

15. Am I thinking big enough? Have you given yourself enough challenge in your goal? Sometimes we don't get our goal because something much greater than we dreamed possible is in store for us.

16. Am I willing to change my direction if it seems appropriate? Am I flexible enough to shift gears if I see that I need to? It is difficult to get started toward a goal if we have little faith in our brake and steering mechanisms. No goal is absolute or forever. Give yourself the right to say no to a goal, to change your mind freely and to feel good about your ability to stay flexible.

17. Would my achieving this goal be good for everyone concerned? Unloving goals are not prospering goals. Is it right for me to have it? Does it really belong to me? We need to know our intentions behind our goals.

18. Does this goal fit my personality, physical strength, psychological makeup, and values? Sometimes an intuitive knowingness cancels our order if it is inconsistent with our basic self. Does this goal fit you?

19. Do I really want what I'm pursuing? Our desires change, but sometimes we've forgotten to update our goals to keep pace. Have you ever wondered why buying something you wanted last year doesn't make you happy now? We need to check our goal list periodically. Maybe we're not getting a certain goal because we no longer want it!

20. Can I name a salary that I feel I'm worthy of? How much are you willing to give yourself.

21. Can I eliminate each negative thought as it comes into my mind? This is the *most important* act of all.

22. Have I released feelings of hurry, worry, and doubt about my progress toward prosperity? One of the main themes of this book is that prosperity thoughts produce prosperous situations. We cannot be hurrying, worrying, and doubting and still be producing true prosperity. We want to do what we can do: choose our goal well; meditate on it; visualize it; affirm it; and allow the experience of having achieved it to fill us. Then we can go about our lives in peace, knowing it is coming. We must allow for 'divine' timing. Many give up too soon. Be patient. Not a single blossom flowers before its time.

23. Am I listening to feedback on my venture? We want to achieve prosperity, not bloody our heads against a solid wall. If you are not being successful, if doors are not opening, pay attention to the signs. This may not be the way for you to go. Forcing creates the opposite effect of what you want. Persistence and patience pay, but when you are on the right path, you know it, you feel it along the way. If you are still finding yourself in situations that make you feel miserable, know that pain is caused by holding on to negative thought. Is there something you need to release? Are there other paths, not explored yet, that may be better suited for your purposes? Negative feedback is an invaluable part of finding the perfect solution. It may be time to check out other possibilities.

24. Am I letting go of being timid? Am I being assertive in situations that call for it? Loving by itself, is not enough in this world. We have the right and duty to protect ourselves. Action based on love, combined with wisdom, gives us all the strength

we need to stand up for ourselves, and to give to others without being 'used'.

25. Am I unattached to the end result? If it would upset you not to achieve prosperity immediately, you will probably benefit by letting go and letting up on yourself. Attachments act as blocks to getting our 'good'. The upset is caused by fear of 'not getting'. We energize this fear with our attachment, thereby creating that which we fear.

26. Do I believe that I deserve and will achieve success in life? We only achieve and maintain what we believe we deserve.

Summary

"You Can Have It If You Really Want It!"

Writing this book has been an exciting adventure for me, and a concrete example of manifestation. I took a year's leave of absence from college teaching to write it, visualizing and affirming from the start its existence in print.

The physical setting in which I chose to write it was also a culmination of a ten-year-old dream. With my new husband, I moved onto a houseboat in the San Francisco Bay, where most of my twelve-hour composing and typing days were spent out on the deck, enjoying the beautiful surroundings. All of this too came about through visualization, affirmation, and meditation.

Every chapter was a new confrontation with myself, as I found I could write about nothing I had left undone in my own life. Just as in teaching, I could write only about what I was living. Although little of what I have written is original in concept, it is so thoroughly integrated into my life that these ideas are no longer a technique outside myself; they are now a way of life. It has been an act of love to review sources and filter information through my own experience, to put it all together in an understandable form so that we may communicate together.

Prosperity consciousness is not something you just get and then have the rest of your life. Once you get it, you never lose it, but we all need to be reminded of it at times. As one of my favorite teachers told me, "I'm teaching you so there will be more of us out there living it — then you can remind me when I forget."

I encourage you to create your daily routine today that supports living the life you fantasize for tomorrow. Here is a morning routine I've found helpful.*

MORNING ROUTINE
Visualizing and Affirming Process

1. **Read goals**
   — of the year, once a month
   — of the month, once a week
   — of the week, every day
   — choose one goal for today to focus on

2. **Visualize goals**
   —from your visualization notebook
   —concentrate on the chosen goal for the day

3. **Affirm weekly affirmations**
   —repeat affirmations *out loud* five times
   —concentrate on the chosen goal for the day

4. **Write affirmation of the day ten times**

5. **Eyes closed process:**
   —Breathe deeply three times, close eyes and relax.
   —See the word 'relax' on the inside of your forehead.
   —Let your whole body 'melt' into the floor or chair as you let go even more.
   —With each exhalation, count down from 10 to 1 and repeat the word, 'deeper'.

---

*Prospering Naturally, a tape leading you through a morning and evening meditation process is available through Whatever Publishing.

—When totally relaxed, non-verbally:
—Affirm your oneness with universal energy.
—Thank infinite intelligence for all you already have.
—Forgive all who have offended you; include your-self
—Declare the negative attitude you are prepared to give up today.
—Affirm your goals of the week 'as if' they had already happened.
—Visualize your goals of the week 'as if' they were already yours.
—Feel *now* how you will feel when your goals are manifested.
—Finish with: "This or something better, with good for all concerned."
—Allow your mind to become still and quiet — remain in concentrated quiet listening.
—Count up from 1 to 10, repeating, "Every day in every way I am feeling better and better," with each breath.
—Open your eyes, feeling alive, awake, enthusiastic to do the work that only you can do to manifest your dreams, feeling assured of success.

Keep your visualization notebook with your yearly, monthly, and weekly goal sheets all together where you do your daily inner work.

This whole process is based upon the following five key thoughts that you may want to remind yourself of:

1. By daily thanking the universe for all the love and good that you already have in your life, you are acknowledging your oneness with universal energy, and the wheels are set in motion to manifest your desires automatically.

2. By concentrating on choosing wisely what you want, not only are you going to be satisfied, but you are willing to realize the consequences and are ready to pay the price for what you want.

3. When you can relax with a quiet mind, you have access to another reality of the higher self. This inner communication is your real work of life. Your outer work is but a reflection of this inner work.

4. Meditation is the means of consulting with your higher self who is available at all times, and knowledge-able on all issues concerning you. When you stay in meditation long enough to:
>   a. ask for direction
>   b. visualize your desires
>   c. affirm with feeling that the goals are yours
>   d. listen with focused awareness

you receive the insights guiding you to your next step.

5. Your ability to give and to forgive are the gifts from infinite intelligence which allow you to open up recep-tively to the bounty of the universe.

EVENING ROUTINE

An evening routine is equally important. Ten minutes before falling asleep:

1. Review your day
Are there incidents you need to 'repair'? If so, visualize yourself going through that incident, handling it just the way you wish you had done it. Then release it.

2. **Review your most important goal**
   Give instruction to your Inside Awareness to bring this goal into being with good for all concerned.

3. **Ask for dreams with clear messages**
   Keep your dream journal handy to record important feeling dreams with messages about your life situations.

4. **Give thanks to the universe for a good night's restful sleep.**

Fortunately, we will never unravel the infinite mysteries of life, so there will be no end to the fun of trying to. With these exercises, routines, and new ways of thinking, we are learning to chart our course, going with the tide of universal energy, guaranteed to take us to whatever is best for us. The energy focused by the subconscious manifests in so many ways, with no barriers in time or space to stop it, that we must always be prepared for the unexpected ways our dreams are realized.

Once you have awakened to your true nature, your real purpose, and have an appreciation of all the opportunities of abundance around you, you have also awakened your power to create more than you need of everything in your life. Now that you know you will succeed because you have the tools to assure that success, you are ready to expect everything and know that *you already have it all.*

Enjoy!

Keys to Prosperity

214 / *Prospering Woman*

Here are a few of the books I have found to be particularly helpful in the development of a prosperity consciousness. I have listed them in five categories: Mental, Physical, Emotional, Spiritual and Financial Prosperity.

Mental Prosperity

Mental prosperity is the foundation of all other prosperity. It is opening our minds to the wisdom of cosmic consciousness. It is allowing the transformation that takes place once we realize who we are and our role in the universe as conscious creatures. When we know who we are, it follows naturally that we are able to receive what we want.

The Roots of Consciousness, Psychic Liberation Through History, Science and Experience by Jeffrey Mishlove. Random House, Bookworks 1979. A provocative, comprehensive study of consciousness and the powers of the mind. This is a well-documented, scholarly approach to consciousness.

The Aquarian Conspiracy, Personal and Social Transformation in the 1980's by Marilyn Ferguson. J.P. Tarcher, Inc., L.A. 1980. Invaluable reference book for understanding what's happening in the transformation of human consciousness.

The Metaphoric Mind by Bob Samples. Addison-Wesley, 1976.

Exploring the Crack in the Cosmic Egg by Joseph Chilton Pearce. Pocket Books, N.Y. 1974.

Experiences in Visual Thinking by Robert McKim. Brooks/Cole, Monterey, 1972. A book designed to help you to be a more flexible, productive thinker utilizing the subconscious as well as the conscious mind.

The Experience of Insight by Joseph Goldstein. Unity, 1976.

The Natural Mind by Andrew Weil. Houghton-Mifflin, 1972.

Mind as Healer, Mind as Slayer by Kenneth R. Pelletier. Delta, 1977. Recommended for understanding the relationship of human consciousness to stress.

The Science of Mind by Ernest Holmes. Dodd, Mead & Co., New York, 1938. Prophet for the new age by his early recognition of the role of mind action in creating physical reality.

The Edinburgh Lectures on Mental Science by Thomas Troward. Dodd, Mead & Co., New York, 1909. Very deep, penetrating thinker.

The Path of Action by Jack Schwarz. E.P. Dutton, New York, 1977. He writes of the creative source within you — the spirit that flows through you — the source of prosperity.

The Master Game by Robert de Ropp. Dell, 1967. A demystified version of Oespensky. This is a great book for looking at purpose in life. The master game, of course, is self-awareness.

Psychic Discoveries Behind the Iron Curtain by Sheila Ostrander and Lynn Schroeder. Bantam Books, 1970.

The Lazy Man's Guide to Enlightenment by Thaddeus Golas. Seed Center, 1971.

Sixty Seconds to Mind Expansion by Harold Cook and Joel Davitz. Pocket Books, 1976.

Acres of Diamonds by Russell H. Conwell Spire Books, Fleming H. Revell Co., N.J. 1979. A classic among prosperity thinkers. Your golden opportunity is wherever you are.

Open Your Mind to Prosperity by Catherine Ponder. Unity Books, Mo. 1971. Simply written, religious descriptions of the process of getting what you want in life through love and right living.

Brain Mind Bulletin, P.O. Box 42211, L.A., Ca. 90042. A two-page monthly bulletin. Has information on the latest scientific research and breakthroughs on understanding conscious evolution and the role of consciousness as an energy force.

Consciousness East and West by Kenneth Pelletier and Charles Garfield. Colophon, 1976. Includes an extensive and valuable bibliography on the study of consciousness.

Paths to Power / A Woman's Guide From First Job to Top Executive by Natasha Josephowitz, Ph. D. Addison-Wesley, Mass. 1980.

Physical Prosperity

Physical prosperity is creating the healthy, vibrant, beautiful body we all want. There is no one standard for what this means. Only you determine what you want from your physical body. Here are some books to help you achieve it.

Workout Book by Jane Fonda. Simon & Schuster 1981. An inspiring book to look at, try out and achieve. Written by someone who is obviously a Prospering Woman!

The Pritikin Program for Diet and Exercise by Nathan Pritikin. Grosset & Dunlap, 1979. I personally agree with Pritikin's ideas on cutting way down on sugar, white flour, fat and salt. It's made a big difference in my health. This book has excellent recipes which means you can have a healthy diet that tastes good too.

Awareness Through Movement by Moche Feldenkrais. Harper & Row, 1972.

The Massage Book by George Downing. Random House, 1972. Prosperity is exchanging a wonderful massage with a loving friend.

Our Bodies, Our Selves. Simon & Schuster, 1973.

The Healing Mind: You Can Cure Yourself Without Drugs by Irving Oyle. Celestial Arts, 1975.

Getting Clear by Anne Kent Rush. Random House 1973.

For Yourself, the Fulfillment of Female Sexuality by Lonnie Garfield Barbach. Anchor Books/Doubleday, N.Y., 1976.

Are You Confused? by Paavo Airola, PH. D., N. D. Health Plus, Ariz., 1971. Physical prosperity demands that we become aware of and follow a nutritious food plan.

Aerobics For Women by Mildred Cooper and Ken Cooper, M.D. Bantam Books, N.Y. 1977. Exercise programs for women of all ages doing common, everyday activities such as walking, running, climbing stairs, etc.

Arica Psycho-calisthenics by Oscar Ichazo. Simon & Schuster, N.Y., 1976. This is my favorite set of exercises. Uses movement combined with breath to align mind, body and emotions. It is a systematic approach to maintaining a supple, spontaneously receptive mind-body.

Wholistic Dimensions in Healing, a Resource Guide by Leslie J. Kaslof. Doubleday Dolphin, N.Y., 1978.

The Relaxation Response by Herbert Benson, M.D. Avon, N.Y., 1975. An excellent resource for understanding the physical benefits of relaxation.

The Relaxation and Stress Reduction Workbook by Martha Davis, PH.D., Matthew McKay, Ph.D. and Elizabeth Robbins Eshelman. New Harbinger, Richmond, Ca., 1980.

Emotional Prosperity

Emotional prosperity happens when we align our feelings with our mental, physical, spiritual, financial goals, and achieve them. As we know our purpose in life, expand our ability to love, become able to say yes and no and feel good about ourselves in the process, experience a positive attitude toward ourselves and others, and feel comfortable with our independence, we are developing our emotional prosperity.

These are a few of the books offering clarity on how to become more emotionally prosperous.

How to Be Your Own Best Friend by Mildred Newman and Bernard Berkowitz. Random House, 1971.

Gestalt Self Therapy by Muriel Schiffman. Self Therapy Press, Menlo Park, Ca., 1971.

Portraits of Loneliness and Love by Clark Moustakas. Prentice-Hall, 1974.

No One is to Blame by Bob Hoffman. Science and Behavior Books, Palo Alto, Ca., 1979. Subtitled "Getting a loving divorce from Mom and Dad," you will learn how to identify and release yourself from the unconscious, crippling messages you got from your parents. The "Quadrinity Process" is a method Hoffman has developed to re-align relationships with parents, and is an antidote to the negative love syndrome most of us developed as kids.

The Angry Book by Theodore Rubin, M.D. Collier-Macmillan, London, 1969.

Love by Leo Buscaglia. Fawcett, N.Y., 1972. To prosper is to love, and to love is to prosper.

Women as Winners by Dorothy Jongeward and Dru Scott. Addison-Wesley Publishing Co. Mass., 1976.

The Way of All Women by Esther Harding. Longmans Green Canada Limited, Toronto, 1970.

The Dynamic Laws of Prosperity by Catherine Ponder. Prentice-Hall, Inc. N.J., 1977. Her books are devoted to understanding the prospering messages of the Bible.

Love is Letting Go of Fear by Gerald G. Jampolsky, M.D. Celestial Arts 1979. Based on the Course in Miracles, this little book can go with you anywhere and provide the stimulus for hours of contemplation on what emotional prosperity is all about.

Pulling Your Own String by Dr. Wayne Drer. Avon, N.Y., 1977.

Intimacy, the Essence of Male and Female by Shirley Luthman. Nash Publishing, L.A., 1972.

The Magical Child Within You by Bruce Davis, Ph.D. Celestial Arts, Millbrae, Ca. 1977. Prosperity is the result of our creative ideas — the playground of our child within.

The Transparent Self by Sidney Jourard. Van Nostrand, 1964.

The New Assertive Woman by Lynn Z. Bloom and Karen Coburn and Joan Peralman. Dell, N.Y., 1975.

Power From Within by Sheila Johnson, Marguerite Craig and Mary Lautner. Proactive Press, Box 296, Berkeley, 1976.

Ability to Love by Allan Fromme, Wilshire. A book that was personally important to me in discovering the process we all go through in learning to love. Helps to explain why some relationships aren't working.

Spiritual Prosperity

Spiritual prosperity can be stated the simplest of all — it is finding our oneness with all there is. When we experience unity we then realize that that which we desire is not separate from us. I recommend these books for further understanding of this principle.

Emerson's Essays, intro. by Irwin Edman. Apollo Editions, Crowell Co., N.Y. 1926. Emerson is not only one of the greatest thinkers, he's one of the most outstanding prosperity thinkers we have ever produced. Reading him you feel renewed, inspired and begin to believe in yourself as a naturally prospering being.

You Are the World by J. Krishnamurti. Harper & Row, N.Y. 1972. The message is in the title. Penetrating discussion on the role of thought in creating reality. He will definitely make you think.

The Tao of Physics by Fritjof Capra. Shambhala, Boulder, 1975. Quantum physics is proving we are all part of the same whole.

Footprints on the Path by Eileen Caddy. Findhorn Publications, Forress, Scotland, 1976. A beautiful, inspiring book by one of the principle founders of Findhorn, an "intentional" community in Scotland. Read it for greater understanding of how to be more in touch with your own inner guidance — your true source of prosperity.

How to Meditate by Lawrence LeShan. Bantam Books, N.Y., 1979. Meditation is one of the most powerful tools we can use for achieving prosperity.

Phenomenon of Man by Teilhard De Chardin. Harper & Row. Evolution is first and foremost, he says, the evolution of the psychic. A "nomad of science" in search of the secret — our rightful place in the scheme of nature. He concluded that all matter is developing toward the phenomenon of consciousness — the only reason for existence.

The Laws of Manifestation by David Spangler. Findhorn Foundation, Forres, Scotland, 1975. A discussion of the natural principles of manifesting — translating energy from one level to another — "making clear to sight or mind." From a spiritual point of view, love is seen as the attracting energy that pulls to each person whatever material, physical change or help needed for that individual's growth.

Prosperity by Charles Fillmore. Unity Books, Missouri, 1936.

Financial Prosperity

Financial prosperity is having the means — money and other resources — to carry out our dreams. Financial prosperity is an integral part of our fulfilled nature, and is a natural result of having pursued our mental, physical, emotional and spiritual prosperity. Here are some excellent books to develop your consciousness of money and financial planning.

Personal Money Management by Bailard, Biehl and Kaiser. Science Research Association, 1977.

The New Money Dynamics by Venita Von Caspel. Reson Publishing Co., Virginia 1978.

The Money Book by Sylvia Porter. Avon Books, 1976.

Complete Estate Planning Guide by Robert Brosterman. McGraw-Hill, Mentor Books, 1979.

The Only Investment Guide You'll Ever Need by Andrew Tobias. Bantam Books, N.Y. 1979.

How to Prosper During the Coming Bad Years by Howard J. Ruff. Warner Books, N.Y., 1979.

Think and Grow Rich by Napoleon Hill. Prentice-Hall, Canada, 1966.

The Greatest Secret in the World by Og Mandino. Bantam Books, N.Y., 1978.

New Profits from the Monetary Crisis by Harry Browne. Warner Books, 1978.

Dunn & Bradstreet's Guide to Your Investments by C. Colburn Hordy. Thomas Crowell, N.Y., 1982.

MoneyLove by Jerry Gillies. Warner Publishing, 1981.
Also Read!

Money Magazine
Changing Times
Wall Street Journal

Specific Techniques

The following books are recommended for information on a variety of techniques helpful in achieving prosperity:
Techniques for visualizing
Techniques for affirming
Techniques for working through conflict between goals
Techniques for making a career choice
Techniques for working with the sub-conscious mind
Techniques for releasing negative thinking

Techniques for visualizing:

Creative Visualization by Shakti Gawain. Whatever Publishing, Inc., Mill Valley, Ca. 1978. If I could only take one book away with me to a deserted island I would take this book. Well written with deep insight, Shakti tells us how everyone can visualize — easily, and thereby create her own prosperity.

Seeing with the Mind's Eye, the History, Techniques and Uses of Visualization by Mike Samuels, M.D. and Nancy Samuels. Random House, 1975. An adventure story of exploring the inner world through visualization. Shows how mental images influence people's lives, and how by holding positive images lives are transformed positively.

Health, Youth and Beauty Through Color Breathing by Linda Clark-Yvonne Martine. Celestial Arts, Millbrae, 1976. Aging is an attitude. We can choose to stay young-looking and feeling. This book describes a wonderful technique for visualizing breath in different colors to facilitate a more youthful appearance.

The Zen of Seeing by Frederick Franck. Vintage Books, Random House, N.Y., 1973. A delightful book on seeing and drawing as meditation. It requires stopping our preoccupations long enough to look at life. Enjoying the moment is a prosperity feeling *always* available. Our ability to visualize internally is greatly enhanced by our ability to "see" physically.

Techniques of using affirmations:

I Deserve Love by Sondra Ray. Les Femmes, Millbrae, Ca., 1976. Outlines in detail how to use affirmation, or autosuggestion for personal fulfillment.

Techniques for working through conflict between goals:

Psychosynthesis by Roberto Assigioli. Penguin Publishing, 1976.

Techniques for helping you make a career choice:

What Color is Your Parachute by Richard Bolles. Ten Speed Press, Berkeley, 1972.

If You Don't Know Where You're Going, You'll Probably End Up Somewhere Else by David P. Campbell. Argus Comm., 1974.

Techniques for reprogramming the sub-conscious:

Silva Mind Control Method by Jose Silva & P. Miele. Pocket Books, 1978.

Living Your Dreams by Gayle Delaney. Harper & Row, S.F., 1979.

Techniques for releasing negative thinking:

Handbook to Higher Consciousness by Ken Keyes. Living Love, 1974. If you know where you want to go, but you feel stuck in where you are, this may be the book for you. Designed to show you how to use your mind creatively — how to release self-defeating attitudes and habits of thought.

Other Books and Tapes
From New World Library

BOOKS

Creative Visualization by Shakti Gawain. This clear and practical guide contains easy-to-use techniques to: feel more relaxed and peaceful, increase your vitality and improve your health, develop your creative talents, create more fulfillment in relationships, reach your career goals, dissolve negative habit patterns, increase your prosperity, and much, much more.

Living in the Light by Shakti Gawain with Laurel King. Shows us a new way of life — becoming a channel for the creative power of the Universe by developing our intuition. Offers both practical and inspirational guidance in expanding our perspective on who we are and what we have the potential to become.

Anybody Can Write by Jean Bryant. Functions as a personalized, self-guided writing workshop that will inspire anyone who is fascinated by the magical power of words on paper. A delightful approach for the non-writer, "blocked" writer and the beginner.

Friends and Lovers—How to Create the Relationships You Want by Marc Allen. An upbeat, knowledgeable, and contemporary guide to living and working with people. Contains a six-step process that is *guaranteed to settle arguments* at home or at work.

Work With Passion—How To Do What You Love For A Living by Nancy Anderson. This highly effective guide will help you master the secrets of finding your niche in life — doing what you love to do and getting paid well for it. *Work With Passion* is filled with inspiring stories of ordinary people who have achieved extraordinary results by following the nine-step program of the author, developed during her years as a highly successful career consultant. This is *the* career book of the 1980's!

Tantra for the West—A Guide to Personal Freedom by Marc Allen. Practical and informative, *Tantra for the West* presents proven principles and techniques to improve the quality of your life in all areas: relationships, sex, work, money, being alone, creativity, food and drink, meditation and yoga, aging and healing, politics, enlightenment and freedom. "A clear and timely book ..."—Marilyn Ferguson.

CASSETTES

Living in the Light. In this powerful hour-long interview, Shakti Gawain reveals the main principles and techniques from her book of the same title, showing us how to connect with our intuition and become a creative channel for personal and planetary transformation.

Stress Reduction and Creative Meditations. Marc Allen guides you through a deeply relaxing, stress-reducing experience on the first side. Side Two contains effective, creative meditations for health, abundance, and fulfilling relationships. Soothing background music by Jon Bernoff.

Creative Visualization. Shakti Gawain guides you through some of the most powerful and effective meditations and techniques from her book.

ORDERING INFORMATION

We invite you to send for a free copy of our full-color catalogue so that you can see our complete selection of books and cassettes.

New World Library
P. O. Box 13257, Northgate Station
San Rafael, CA 94913
(415) 472-2100

ORDER TOLL FREE WITH YOUR VISA/MC
(800) 227-3900
(800) 632-2122 in California

ABOUT THE AUTHOR

Ruth Ross, Ph.D., the daughter of a tenant farmer, decided at an early age that she would never be poor again. She returned to college after her daughters were in school, developed a successful career, completed a doctorate, and achieved her goals of financial independence along the way.

In her writing and teaching, Dr. Ross draws upon 10 years experience as a college counselor/instructor and as a Marriage-Family Therapist. Her college classes on self-discovery emphasize that "attaining what we desire for our financial, physical and mental well-being is not only possible, it is a necessary part of the balance in being human."

An ardent promoter of women's interests, she conducts self-awareness seminars, creating an atmosphere in which participants experience their joy, self-confidence, and sense of prosperity without guilt.

In her private practice, she uses affirmation psychology with visualization techniques to assist women and men to realize their goals and experience the truth that "abundance is a natural state of being."

As founder of "Prospering Naturally," a network of communication consultants that produce seminars for business and private groups, Ruth Ross lectures widely on the subject of "Getting what you want out of life" through self-fulfillment.

For information about her workshops, seminars and key-note talks, write her at 65 B Gate Five Road, Sausalito, CA 94965.